Praise for *Amazing Courage*

"It's one thing to read a book that you enjoy; it's an even more special thing to read a book that you admire! *Amazing Courage* is written with an appreciation for life's simple yet significant moments. It heralds faith in the face of fear and the love between father and son on every page. It's a beautiful read!"

JOSHUA CANIZARO,
Lead Pastor, One Hope Church, and surviving sibling

"Kyle Zunker's *Amazing Courage* meets us in all the places where fear finds us: in the darkness of a deserted highway, in the middle of a swimming pool, in a cancer treatment center. In each of these places (and many others), Zunker demonstrates how faith in a loving God can provide us with the courage we need to meet the challenges life sets before us. Using a series of letters written to support and encourage his father during cancer treatment as a springboard, Zunker confronts some of the moments in his own life when he resisted the power of faith and turned instead to himself for answers. Leaning into God's abiding strength in our moments of weakness should be easy. Zunker explains why it's not, and why the amazing courage that comes to us through our faith in God is a gift that can help us get through life's most difficult moments."

DR. PAMELA JOHNSTON,
Professor of English at Texas Lutheran University, author (Little Lost River), and care partner for husband with Parkinson's Disease

"Using a tapestry of God's word woven with destiny, love, prayer, suffering, endurance, grace, and truth, non-believer turned believer Kyle Zunker has fashioned a reassuring son to dad love story through eighteen letters written during his dad's cancer battle. Apparent in the letters, along with anecdotal stories, is the two-word fatherly guidance from dad to son, 'You belong,' enhancing this moving account of faith over fear."

DR. DAVID JONES,
former Superintendent of Webb CISD, former Trustee of the
Christian School at Castle Hills, and cancer survivor

"The moment we learned our daughter Lily needed a heart transplant, I knew my life would require a new level of faith. And if being Lily's father wasn't enough to challenge me to trust God with the unexpected, losing our newborn son and being diagnosed with thyroid cancer left me with nowhere else to turn but to God. C.S. Lewis once said, 'Relying on God has to begin again every day as if nothing had ever been done.' Through this book built on letters to his father, Kyle drives home the key truth we all need to learn: God is willing and able to help us overcome every challenging circumstance, if only we will have the courage to trust Him."

DAVID HERNANDEZ,
owner of Bexar General Contractors, father of a
#heartwarrior daughter, and bereaved father of a son

AMAZING COURAGE

*Letters to My Father on Conquering
Fear through Faith*

KYLE ZUNKER

For God has not given us a spirit of fear, but of power and of love and of a sound mind.

2 TIMOTHY 1:7 NKJV

A note from the author

THANK YOU FOR supporting my mission to help people conquer fear through faith. Whether you purchased this copy of *Amazing Courage* or received it as a gift, I would like to offer you a free, bonus resource to express my gratitude.

I distilled the lessons discussed in this book into a five-part framework called the 5 Cs to Conquer Fear. Please visit bonus.amazingcouragebook.com to receive a free, one-page summary of the 5 Cs to Conquer Fear.

Gratefully,

CONTENTS

Introduction

I PULLED MY PHONE from my pocket as I walked down the stairs of my apartment's parking garage. I had two missed calls from my father. *That's strange*, I thought as I called him back. I was used to receiving text messages and the occasional missed call from him, but never a double call.

When my father answered, his voice stopped me. There was something in it I had never heard in twenty-nine years as his son: His voice was choked with fear. I leaned back against the concrete wall of the garage and slid down to the ground as my father spoke. Some phone calls I will never forget. This was one. He had esophageal cancer.

Two thoughts hit my mind as I sat, stunned, on the concrete floor. The first was treatment. I admired my father as a man of action and hard work. Whatever the treatment regimen was, I knew he could handle it.

The second was faith. Three years earlier, I had chosen faith in Jesus Christ, and it changed my life. I had spent years as an atheist. Not an "I'm on the fence about it" or an "I don't really think about it" atheist—a steadfast, theist-debating, Christian-ridiculing atheist. I saw myself as more intelligent, more pragmatic, and far more fun than religious people who were confined by the rules of their antiquated beliefs.

But as highly as I regarded myself, there was one thing I knew I was not: at peace. I had doubled down my bet on happiness coming from my next achievement over and over, until I busted. My life looked to others like a dream but was really a secret, lonely nightmare. I was living in constant fear—of failure, of illness, of judgment, and even of fear itself.

The restoration faith brought to my life was miraculous, as I will discuss in this book. But despite the importance of this change in my life, I had never discussed faith or fear with my father. After nearly three decades of sticking to the comfortable topics of sports and career in my conversations with him, faith had become an unapproachable subject. Like still water in the winter, ice too thick to break had formed over that conversation—until I got the call. When my father told me about his cancer diagnosis, no amount of ice could stop me. I believed he could experience the same restoration I had. I believed faith could save my father.

I wrote eighteen letters about faith to my father during his cancer treatment. They were not sophisticated explications of Scripture or complicated theories of theology. They were short, personal messages of hope sent in love. They were words of encouragement to choose faith over fear. For twenty-nine years, my father repeated two simple words: "You belong." That was his message to me every time I faced a challenge or felt like an outsider.

My letters to him were my attempt to return that love and support, and they worked. They opened new conversations between us. The letters taught me something I did not expect: Admitting we feel fear produces strength, not weakness.

I decided to turn those letters into a book because I want to tell as many people as possible about the life-transforming power to choose faith over fear. The eighteen letters I wrote to my father are its backbone. They are real and raw. The hand-written originals traveled from San Antonio, Texas, to Atlanta, Georgia, the old-fashioned way—via snail mail, in white envelopes with postage stamps. I wrote each letter on the date noted, often in the span of an hour, after a morning run and before heading into work. I decided against revising the letters in the process of writing this book because I want to show what choosing faith looked like in the moment when I had the most to fear.

I paired the letters with stories from my life, which I wrote later, after my father's battle with cancer. Each story regards a lesson I learned about faith and fear and serves as a reflection on the letter it follows. I did not always appreciate these moments in my life as lessons about faith in real time; several of them are from my years as an atheist. But I think God, sitting outside of time, feels no constraint to provide us with the lesson in the same moment as the problem for which we need it. I believe God may show us at ten years old the answer to a question we do not ask until we are twenty-nine.

This book is not a typical memoir or treatise about faith. Each chapter is a distinct directive on the path of choosing faith over fear. Although the letters are in chronological order, the stories are not, because this book is not a biography. It is a guide to overcoming fear and a real-life case study of faith in action. It is not theory for academics; it is a call to action for people in pain. I wrote this book for anyone who is sick or hurting and everyone who is tired of letting fear rob them of their lives. We do not have to linger in the shadow of fear. We have a choice. We can choose faith.

Let me clear the air regarding the title, *Amazing Courage*. The point of this book is not that I am amazingly courageous. It is just the opposite. Faith in God transformed me from someone so gripped by fear I could not get through a day without self-medicating to someone who litigates multimillion-dollar lawsuits for a living. John Newton got it right when he penned his immortal hymn, "Amazing Grace." The definition of "amazing" is "causing astonishment, great wonder, or surprise." Newton's hymn has resonated with millions over the centuries because it captures the state in which God's grace leaves its recipients. God's courage works the same way. It will surprise you, astonish you, and leave you in wonder. The courage you receive through choosing faith will literally amaze you.

FAITH IS NOT RESERVED FOR PEOPLE WHO ARE CERTAIN ABOUT GOD.

If I had picked up this book ten years ago, I would not have read it. If I had seen the words "faith in Jesus Christ" in the fourth paragraph of the introduction, I would have rolled my eyes as I put the book back on the shelf. I am sure some people will feel the same way. I want those people to know this is not a book about shaming atheists or making people feel bad for having doubts. I am a former atheist who still struggles with doubts, and I wrote the book.

Faith is not reserved for people who are certain about God. We each get an invitation to choose faith. I rejected mine day after day for years. But I am beyond thankful I accepted it when I did because it changed my life. It brought me peace more tranquil than I could understand and joy more durable than I had ever known. It enabled me to achieve goals I thought were impossible and to love others more deeply than I ever cared to. But more than anything else, it gave me the courage to conquer fear when I got the phone call I never saw coming.

July 30, 2019

HEY POPS —   1/2

DESPITE ALL OF THE WONDERFUL INSTANT COMMUNICATION TECHNOLOGY, I THINK THERE EXISTS A UNIQUE POWER IN HAND-WRITTEN LETTERS. THE GOOD NEWS ABOUT CHRIST, FOR EXAMPLE, WAS RECORDED IN HAND-WRITTEN LETTERS FROM THE APOSTLES. I HOPE THESE LETTERS HAVE POWER FOR YOU.

AS OUR FAMILY ENTERS THIS TRYING SEASON, I AM REMINDED OF SOMETHING YOU TAUGHT ME AS A BOY: THE ONE THING NO ONE CAN TAKE FROM YOU IS YOUR POSITIVE ATTITUDE. YOU TAUGHT ME THAT WE DO NOT ALWAYS CONTROL WHAT HAPPENS TO US, BUT ALWAYS CONTROL OUR RESPONSE

THIS LESSON REMINDS ME OF ROMANS 8:38-39, IN WHICH THE APOSTLE PAUL WROTE:

> AND I AM CONVINCED THAT NOTHING CAN EVER SEPARATE US FROM GOD'S LOVE. NEITHER DEATH NOR LIFE, NEITHER ANGELS NOR DEMONS, NEITHER OUR FEARS FOR TODAY NOR OUR WORRIES ABOUT TOMORROW — NOT EVEN THE POWERS OF HELL CAN SEPARATE US FROM GOD'S LOVE.
> NO POWER IN THE SKY ABOVE OR IN THE EARTH BELOW — INDEED NOTHING IN ALL CREATION WILL EVER BE ABLE TO SEPARATE US FROM THE LOVE OF GOD REVEALED IN OUR LORD CHRIST JESUS.

Those verses are so powerful. There is nothing, without exception or qualification, that can separate us from God. People say the world is a bad place because good things can be taken from you; I say it is good because the best cannot. Knowing this, we can choose hope over despair, courage over fear, and love over hate, even in this trial.

We will fight together; together, we will win. With a son's love for his father,

CHAPTER ONE

Take Control

Summer 2000 — Comanche, Texas

MY TOES GRIPPED the grit of the board as my knees trembled. My hands were latched to the steel rails on both sides. I looked over my shoulder and down the ladder I had just climbed. It was much farther from the diving board to the ground than it had been from the ground to the diving board. I turned forward, released the rails, and shuffled down the board. When I reached the end, I craned my neck over the edge and looked down at the vast expanse below me. My heart pounded. *Just jump,* I told myself.

WHEN I WAS ten years old, my parents, brother, and I went to a family reunion in Comanche, Texas. We stayed at an old, horseshoe-style motel, the kind where the doors to all the rooms face in toward the parking lot. Two things about the motel room stand out in my memory.

One was the sweltering air in the room as the wimpy window AC unit lost its battle with the Texas summer heat, even after the sun went down. The other was waking up to my mother screaming, then turning to see a frisbee-sized tarantula crawling up the wall. We checked out of that motel, and I do not remember where we stayed after that. I suppose it was a nondescript room without five-pound arachnids on the walls.

The only other place I remember from the family reunion is the town's outdoor public pool with its mammoth high dive. I am sure Comanche, like other small Texas towns, is full of wonderful people. But for me, Comanche will always be home to the world's largest tarantula and tallest high dive.

If you never attended a family reunion as a kid, please let me explain how it goes. You ride in the car for several hours with your parents and younger brother, headed somewhere you have never been. When you get there, your parents talk to a lot of people you do not know and make you say hello to them. These people say things like, "Last time I saw you, you were in diapers," or, "I'm going to stack books on your head to keep you from growing."

You laugh nervously and look around for other kids who do not look too mean, but you do not see any. All you see are old people playing dominoes and ladies wearing matching yellow shirts. Then, just when things look desperate, your parents take you to the public pool. Sometimes it is a lake, river, or beach. The point is, it is the summer oasis where you and twenty other kids will spend the next few days.

I remember seeing the high dive as soon as we entered through the gate. It was in the far back corner, towering over the deep end. I had a lot of time to admire it as my mother rubbed a thick coat of sunscreen onto my pasty skin. I watched kid after kid bound up the ladder, bounce out to the edge of the board, and soar. It seemed like ages before they hit the water.

I had seen a high dive before, but I had never considered jumping. This time was different. I was a big kid now and wanted in on the action. I was going to jump.

I checked my steps as I walked across the pool deck toward the towering structure. Every kid in Texas knows you step only on the wet spots or, if there are none, dunk your feet into the edge of the pool every few steps, unless you want to leave the soles of your feet charred on the ground behind you.

When I got to the base of the ladder, I had to wait for the kid who was already on the board. I looked back at my mother, who was talking to my aunts, and at my brother, who was floating in the shallow end. I thought about my friends back home. I was going to be a different kid when I saw them next.

A loud splash snapped my attention back. It was my turn. I took each rung with care, looking down at my feet as I climbed. After a few steps, I thought I must be near the top, but looked up and saw more rungs. I carried on, looking down as the ground disappeared below me. I scrambled over the last rung and stood up. My toes gripped the gritty board and my hands latched on to the rails. The wind gusted over my shivering body. I crept forward and craned my neck over the edge. *Are you serious? I'll never survive a fall from this height.* I looked down and saw my mother smiling. *Just jump,* I told myself. *The other kids jumped, and they were fine.*

It was no use. My heart pounded as I backed away and stepped down the ladder. The next kid was already halfway up and had to climb down to move out of my way.

YOU HAVE A lot of time to think before you jump from a high dive. As you walk around the pool, you can examine the landing area, making sure the water is deep enough. As you climb the ladder rung by rung, you can look around, checking to see who is present to impress or disappoint. As you inch out onto the board, you can look down, evaluating whether the jump looks safe.

At all these points, even with your toes hanging from the end of the board, you have time and options. You can turn around and climb down the ladder. You can decide you are not ready for the jump, resolve to take swim lessons, or try to build up your confidence with small jumps from the pool deck. You can promise yourself that one day—but not today—you will make the jump.

Life is the same way. We have high dives we point to and say, "One day, I am going to jump from that." I had a massive high dive in my life. I had been planning to write a book about faith for years. I spent my late teens and early twenties on a bender of self-indulgence, an atheist who wanted to prove I was the most important person in the world. I wanted to party the hardest, make the highest grades, work the longest hours, and say the cleverest things. Years of this narcissistic effort left me anxious, depressed, and terrified.

Then, at my most hopeless point, God saved me. I wanted to help people find the hope I had found by steering them away from the direction I had wandered. I had dreamed, brainstormed, planned, outlined, and even started writing, but backed down. I had circled the pool, checked the water, climbed the ladder, walked to the edge of the board, and bounced up and down, but turned back.

It was not for lack of passion or clarity; I felt desire and conviction to write my book. But every time I got to the end of my diving board, I let fear—the fear of failure, the fear my book would not be original, important, or well-written enough, the fear I was not a good enough person to write about faith—paralyze me and send me walking down the ladder in defeat.

Then, my father told me he had cancer. I will never forget the phone call; it was the first time I ever heard fear in my father's voice. And when I heard it, my paralyzing fear went away. I started writing letters to him about faith. I was not concerned with whether they were original, important, or well-written. I was concerned with whether they would help my father find truth, faith, and peace. I was concerned with whether I was encouraging my father and showing him that hope—the real, infallible, and unassailable hope of the Gospel—exists at all times for all people, including cancer patients.

The way I think about fear changed when I started writing the letters. I stopped being afraid of so many things in life when I started being afraid I would miss my role in God's will. I think that is what fearing God means: trusting His will so deeply that going against it is the only thing to fear.

It means choosing to risk the jump rather than standing on the diving board until it is too late, choosing to risk failure rather than shrinking from the moment for which God has built and trained us. It is neither paralyzing nor intimidating, but liberating. It gives us the power to choose. It gives us the power to take action.

FEARING GOD MEANS: TRUSTING HIS WILL SO DEEPLY THAT GOING AGAINST IT IS THE ONLY THING TO FEAR.

We do not have to let fear control us. God tells us not to fear anything, even sickness and death, because nothing can separate us from His love, and He has worked all things for our good. Having faith in God's indestructible love does not prevent us from feeling fear; it allows us to conquer it. And there is no better feeling than the joy of conquering fear.

It was the feeling I had that day at the Comanche public pool when I climbed back up the ladder. The feeling of my iron resolve battling my trembling legs until the moment I closed my eyes and jumped. The feeling of my stomach spinning as I fell, fast and free. The feeling of the cool water engulfing me, and the feeling of excitement as I swam back to the surface to look over at my family. But more than anything, it was the feeling of my joy as I climbed out of the pool. I never want to let fear rob me of that joy again. Fear can scare me, but it cannot stop me.

GOD'S WORD ABOUT FEAR:

✝ *And I am convinced that nothing can ever separate us from God's love. Neither death nor life, neither angels nor demons, neither our fears for today nor our worries about tomorrow—not even the powers of hell can separate us from God's love. No power in the sky above or in the earth below—indeed, nothing in all creation will ever be able to separate us from the love of God that is revealed in Christ Jesus our Lord.*

ROMANS 8:38–39 NLT

✝ *Whoever fears the LORD has a secure fortress,*
and for their children it will be a refuge.
The fear of the LORD is a fountain of life,
turning a person from the snares of death.

PROVERBS 14:26–27 NIV

✝ *Have I not commanded you? Be strong and courageous. Do not be afraid; do not be discouraged, for the LORD your God will be with you wherever you go.*

JOSHUA 1:9 NIV

Hey Pops—

I think sometimes waiting to learn what challenge lies ahead is more difficult than the challenge itself. I imagine this is especially true for a man of action like you. Perhaps the wait for a plan to execute or the uncertainty of how you will respond to an unfamiliar situation seems like an impossible burden.

Do you remember the summer of 2004? I do, vividly. You spent the decade leading up to that summer encouraging me after countless strikeouts at the plate. You were not only at my games, but at my practices and the batting cages. I was not a good hitter; there is no way around that. But that did not stop you from somehow getting me on to a traveling select team in 2004. Again, I struggled hitting. Again, you supported and encouraged me. The idea that I could ever hit a homerun was, in my mind, ludicrous. I was terrified of failure at the plate; hitting a homerun was not possible. Except it was. On Father's Day of 2004, with you encouraging me from the stands, I hit a homerun over dead center field. I remember rounding second base at a sprint before I realized it was over the fence. I remember the excitement,

PRIDE, AND CONFIRMATION IN YOUR EYES WHEN YOU CAME TO THE DUGOUT TO CONGRATULATE ME. THAT WAS ONE OF THE MOST IMPORTANT DAYS OF MY LIFE. WITH THE SUPPORT OF MY FATHER, I LEARNED I COULD DO THINGS THAT SEEMED IMPOSSIBLE.

POPS, YOU HAVE A HEAVENLY FATHER SUPPORTING YOU AND HE WANTS YOU TO KNOW THAT NOTHING IS IMPOSSIBLE. IN PHILIPPIANS 4:12-13, THE APOSTLE PAUL WROTE:

I KNOW HOW TO LIVE ON ALMOST NOTHING OR WITH EVERYTHING. I HAVE LEARNED THE SECRET OF LIVING IN EVERY SITUATION, WHETHER IT IS WITH FULL STOMACH OR EMPTY, WITH PLENTY OR LITTLE. FOR I CAN DO EVERYTHING THROUGH CHRIST, WHO GIVES ME STRENGTH.

IF YOUR CHALLENGE SEEMS LIKE MORE THAN YOU CAN HANDLE, DO NOT TRY TO HANDLE IT ALONE. PRAY AND DRAW STRENGTH THROUGH CHRIST. NOTHING IS IMPOSSIBLE.

WE WILL FIGHT TOGETHER;
TOGETHER, WE WILL WIN.
WITH A SON'S LOVE FOR
HIS FATHER,

CHAPTER TWO

Do Impossible

August 21, 2021 – Hope Pass, Colorado

I STEPPED UNDER THE tent to get out of the rain and looked around. Thirty to forty other runners were there with me. A few were refilling their packs with water and food, but most were sitting in chairs, staring at the ground with lifeless eyes. Some were crying. I knew how they felt. We had been running for more than thirteen hours, had traversed fifty miles, and had just climbed and descended a three-thousand-foot mountain pass. Now, we had to turn around and do it all over again—and we had to do it fast. We had just four hours to make it back over Hope Pass to beat the next cutoff.

IN 2020, I signed up to run the 2021 edition of the Leadville Trail 100, a 100-mile foot race through the Rocky

Mountains. The race features more than 15,000 thousand feet of climbing, but what makes it unique is not the elevation gain; it is the altitude. The highest point, Hope Pass, stands at 12,508 feet above sea level. The lowest point, Twin Lakes, is still a staggering 9,219 feet above sea level. Most of the 100-mile race takes place at over 10,000 feet in altitude, making Leadville, known as the "Race Across the Sky," one of the highest-altitude ultraruns in the world. The air at that height is thin and dry and has about two-thirds the oxygen concentration of air at sea level.

Shortly after I signed up for Leadville, my wife, Hannah, and I moved from San Antonio to New Orleans, a city that is charming, unique, authentic, delicious, fun, and more. But there is one thing it is not—a good training base for mountain running. The city sits at sea level with almost no naturally occurring elevation change. There are a few man-made hills in the zoo and park that reach staggering heights like twenty-seven feet. Otherwise, the pancake-flat city of New Orleans is a bowl of hot, heavy, humid air, the closest you can get to living in a pot of gumbo. It is hard to imagine a place more different from Leadville, Colorado.

I trained all year on the streetcar lines, levee, and track around Audubon Park. To encourage myself, I read articles about how high humidity is supposed to be a good proxy for altitude. It did not feel that way to me. I went to Colorado three weeks ahead of the race to acclimatize and practice on the course. I may as well have been on another planet running on those mountain trails. My oxygen levels were too low. I could not run more than a few minutes before hitting my heart rate threshold indicating it was time to walk. After almost a full three weeks in the mountains, just days before the race, I started to feel ever so slightly acclimated, but there was no time for a training run at that point. After eight months of training, I was in the two-day rest period before the race. I was going to need a miracle to get to the finish line on race day.

It was cold and dark when I joined the crowd at the starting line. It was 3:50 am, ten minutes before the start. I prayed with Hannah, then went over my race plan in my mind as someone sang the national anthem. The race started at 4:00 am on the dot. I stuck to my plan and walked when my heartrate hit 155 beats per minute, then started running again when it dropped to 135. I had crafted that approach in the intense heat and humidity at sea level. It had served me well all summer, but it did not translate to altitude on race day. Within a few miles of the start, I was well behind the pack. I stayed calm. *It's just the start, and it's a long race. Stick to your plan. You aren't going too slow; everyone else is going too fast.* I told myself these things all the way to the first checkpoint at mile twelve, where I arrived thirty minutes behind my race plan. I started to worry. By the time I was approaching the big checkpoint at Mile 38 in Twin Lakes, I was panicking.

It was near 1:00 pm. I had been able to see the town of Twin Lakes for miles as I followed switchbacks down the side of Mount Elbert. I heard the voices of crews and spectators cheering on the athletes ahead of me, a cruel reminder of how far behind I was. For the past hour, all I had thought about was the time slipping by and the mysterious heartburn raging in my throat. When I crossed the timing line and entered the checkpoint, I could not hold it back—the pain, frustration, and fear boiled over inside me and came leaking out of my eyes. I wiped the tears off my cheeks as Hannah greeted me and guided me to our wagon and lawn chairs. I sat down and composed myself enough to speak.

"Write the miles of the checkpoints and cutoff times on my arm," I said. I had not memorized the cutoff times. They were not supposed to be an issue for me according to the ten-page race plan I spent days writing and revising. But I was over an hour behind my plan after completing just one-third of the race. The old race plan was out; the new race plan was written on my right forearm in sharpie: get to the checkpoints by the cutoff times. I studied the new plan, checked my watch, and did the quick math. It was not good. I had left myself no room for error on the most difficult portion of the course. Standing before me was a literal mountain, Hope Pass. I had to climb it, run down the backside to the fifty-mile checkpoint, then turn around, climb back up the mountain, and run back down. I needed to be back in this chair in less than nine hours.

I got up, put my vest back on, grabbed my trekking poles and two sweet potato tacos wrapped in foil, and headed out. I felt reenergized as I ran through the town street lined with spectators and across the flat field to the head of the mountain trail. When I started the climb and slowed to a hike, I unwrapped one of the tacos. I took a bite and chewed. I tried to swallow but could not.

I pulled off the trail a few steps. Maybe I needed to focus on eating. Maybe I was too exhausted for the coordination of hiking and eating at the same time. I directed all my attention to swallowing the food in my mouth, but nothing happened. I simply could not swallow. Some subconscious part of my brain had decided my stomach was not accepting any more solid food, and there was nothing I could do to convince it otherwise. I spit out the chewed-up mouthful of sweet potatoes. The next aid station was at the top of the mountain. I would have to finish the climb without any calories.

I pushed onward and upward. I fell in behind a woman moving about the same pace as I was, and we stuck together for a while. She had a message to other runners written on the back of her calves: "Tell me your why." The words were directly in front of my eyes since she was ahead and uphill of me.

I wanted to tell her my why. I wanted to show her the words written on my forearm. Not the cutoff times on my right arm, but the words on my left arm, the two words my father always told me: "You belong." I wanted to tell her about the charity I was running for, the people who had donated to my campaign, and the poem titled "Why" that I wrote during my long training runs in the oppressive New Orleans humidity.

But I did not. I was using every ounce of energy to push my body up the mountain. I was too tired, too hungry, and too desperate to beat the clock to talk to her. We pushed forward in silence, supporting each other with our mutual presence and continued effort.

I reached the checkpoint at the summit just before the next cutoff. I drank some broth and a few cups of a caffeine-loaded electrolyte mix. I felt better, which was good because I still had an impossible task ahead of me. I needed to descend the back half of Hope Pass—the steeper half—then turn around and climb back up. And I needed to do it fast.

As soon as I took the first downhill step, I opened it up. Having trained all year in New Orleans, I had little experience running downhill. But I knew I could not hold anything back and still make the cutoff. I moved as fast as I could without falling down the mountain. I passed dozens of other runners on their way down. The runners who were already on their way back up looked bewildered when we crossed paths. I was in the back of the pack, but was running like someone who should be competing for a top-ten finish. My feet and ankles took a beating as I pounded downhill with zero finesse. I checked my watch every few minutes as I approached the bottom.

"You gotta scoot, man. You're not gonna make it," another runner on his way up scoffed as we crossed paths. His words burned in my ears.

The sky darkened, the wind picked up, and hail started to fall as I grinded out the last mile to the checkpoint. The weather mirrored the storm raging in my soul. I was a frenzy of emotions, but I made it to the fifty-mile checkpoint before cutoff.

A light rain had replaced the hail. There was a large tent at the checkpoint, and I stepped under it. The overcast sky made the scene look colorless, like a battlefield hospital in a black-and-white movie. I walked up to the table for another round of the caffeine-loaded electrolyte mix and to refill my vest. One of the other runners under the tent was sobbing as her friend tried to tell her she could make it back over the mountain. I looked around at the rest of the runners under the tent. Their eyes were sunken. Everyone was thinking the same thing. We had to go back over the mountain we just climbed. And there was a good chance we would miss the cutoff, and all that work would be for naught.

WE WERE IN the pain cave: an allegorical place in every endurance event where the amount of pain you feel makes completing the race seem impossible. But I knew a secret about the pain cave, something I had learned running mile after mile through the suffocating summer air of New Orleans. The pain cave is a lie fear tells us. People do not quit long races because of pain. They quit because of fear. Pain comes to us moment by moment; we experience the pain of each step as we take it. But fear is different. Fear makes us feel future pain in the present moment. Fear makes us feel fifty miles worth of pain in every step. We can always push through the pain of the moment, but we cannot handle fifty miles worth of pain in each step. It is too much, so we quit.

This is fear's modus operandi. Fear points ahead and asks, "What if …?," to bring the potential tragedy and pain of the future into the present. Fear is nothing in itself; it is always a shadow of something else. But if we live in that shadow, then we live in the pain as well.

That is fear's power. Fear of illness makes a healthy person sick with anxiety. Fear of poverty makes a wealthy person stress over finances. Fear of heartache makes a person longing for companionship withdraw into isolation. And fear of pain makes a runner quit when he still has miles left in his legs. Fear is a fraud who robs us of today with threats about tomorrow.

But we have a powerful tool against fear's lies. We can do something fear tells us is impossible. That is what I did at the fifty-mile checkpoint. I was more physically exhausted than I had ever been in my life, and the race was only half over. Fear told me I could not make it back up the mountain—probably not at all, and definitely not by the cutoff time. Fear told me I could not handle the pain in my legs for another thirteen hours of running and hiking. Fear told me it was better to quit in the tent than to keep trying and fail on the trail. I did not listen to fear. I drowned its lies in truth.

> FEAR IS A FRAUD WHO ROBS US OF TODAY WITH THREATS ABOUT TOMORROW.

I restocked my vest and headed out. The longest run of my life before that day was fifty miles, so every step moving forward was a new personal record. I ran until the path became too steep and then I hiked. I stared into the ground in front of my face as I climbed. Fear whispered lies, but I spoke truth to myself. I spoke the words my father told me. *You belong. You belong on the course. You belong at the top of the mountain. You belong at the finish line. You belong.* I repeated the words over and over.

I pushed up the slope with my legs and pulled on my trekking poles with my arms. Fear was not whispering to me anymore. I went somewhere it could not follow. There was nothing else in the world but the ground in front me, my pounding heart, and my throbbing muscles. *You belong. You belong. You belong.*

When I reached the summit and looked back over my shoulder at the sun setting in the mountains behind me, I knew I would finish the race. I still had to run more than 40 miles through the mountains in the dark of night, but I had no doubt. I was permitted a pacer once I got back to Twin Lakes, and my running buddy, Davey J, was waiting for me there. He would see me across the finish line. There was nothing ahead of me I could not overcome.

I savored a few more seconds of looking into the sunset before starting down the mountain. I did not want to forget that moment. I knew I would be leaving the race a different person from the one who started it. In the forge of suffering and fearlessly pressing forward into a challenge I thought was impossible, I found something within myself, a part of me that had been suppressed by fear for years, maybe forever. I set that part of myself free on the mountain.

GOD'S WORD ABOUT THE POWER OF FAITH:

✝ *I know how to live on almost nothing or with everything. I have learned the secret of living in every situation, whether it is with a full stomach or empty, with plenty or little. For I can do everything through Christ, who gives me strength.*

PHILIPPIANS 4:12–13 NLT

✝ *For our struggle is not against flesh and blood, but against the rulers, against the authorities, against the powers of this dark world and against the spiritual forces of evil in the heavenly realms. Therefore put on the full armor of God, so that when the day of evil comes, you may be able to stand your ground, and after you have done everything, to stand.*

EPHESIANS 6:12–13 NIV

✝ *He replied, "Because you have so little faith. Truly I tell you, if you have faith as small as a mustard seed, you can say to this mountain, 'Move from here to there,' and it will move. Nothing will be impossible for you."*

MATTHEW 17:20 NIV

Hey Pops —

Do you ever wonder why, throughout history, the family has been the fundamental unit of human community? It does not logically have to be that way; we could have been like some animal species who mate to reproduce but form no families. I think the reason we place so much value on family is the same reason we make some, but not many, deep friendships. The reason is trust. We want to be in community with people we can trust so that we do not spend our lives in the exhausting act of worrying and speculating about peoples' motives. This is, I believe, why we hurt so bad when family or close friend violates our trust.

We could articulate what we are trusting others to do or not do in many different ways, but I think ultimately we trust others to will for our good and not for our bad. This is the exact basis God gives for our trust in Him in Jeremiah 29:11-13, when He spoke to the Israelites in exile:

"For I know the plans I have for you," says the Lord. "They are plans for good and not for disaster, to give you a future and a hope. In those days when you pray, I will listen. If you look for me wholeheartedly, you will find me."

God did not limit these words to people who happen to be enjoying good fortune at that moment. God was speaking through the prophet Jeremiah to the Israelites who were exiled, imprisoned, enslaved, and oppressed in Babylon. Furthermore, unlike family and friends, God is all good and all powerful; he will not break his promises and has the power to fulfill them. You can trust God's promise for a good future full of hope more than you can trust the ground to stay beneath you. Pray to God for a spirit of trust.

We will fight together; together, we will win.
With a son's love for his father,

C H A P T E R   T H R E E

Change Plans

Fall 2013 – Dallas, Texas

I STEPPED INTO THE small elevator and pressed the button for the second floor. The familiar smell and wobbly, slow climb draped a 100-pound dread over my shoulders. I had been giddy with excitement the first time I stepped into the elevator, and the second time, and the third time. But after a few dozen rejections, the elevator had become my private transport to misery. The doors opened, and I stepped out into the career services office. I walked down the hall, past all of the small conference rooms where I had failed over and over. I knocked on the open door of my counselor's office.

"Oh, hey, Kyle. Come on in," he invited.

I closed the door behind me and sat down. He was wearing a friendly, optimistic smile, but I could tell he was concerned. I looked out the window while he looked over my papers on his desk. *What can you possibly do to help me?* I thought to myself.

CONSTRUCTION HAS ALWAYS fascinated me. From as early as I can remember, my father worked in new home construction. He was not a carpenter or electrician. I do not remember ever seeing him use a power tool. He was a people person; he managed teams and sold houses. I spent a lot of time as a child touring construction sites and model houses. I will never forget the smell of a model home, the mix of new carpet and air freshener. My father had a routine when we left model homes at night. He would open the front door and then open the alarm keypad.

"Ok, son. Be still and quiet, or else the alarm will trigger," he would say.

I watched, frozen and silent, as the buttons glowed orange when he touched them. When he finished typing the code, he flipped the white, plastic cover up and pointed outside to the car, and whispered, "Don't make any sounds or the alarm will go off." I would tiptoe out the door and down the walkway, staying silent as I climbed into the back seat and buckled up. I wouldn't dare to talk until my father was in the car with the driver door closed. I am not sure if my father found it funny to watch me or just wanted a few moments of quiet, but he used that trick every time.

Because of my exposure to construction, my first dream job was to be an architect or engineer. I wanted to build bridges and skyscrapers. But my father saw only two potential careers for me: doctor or lawyer.

"You can be anything you want to be, any type of doctor or lawyer you want," my father often said.

We did not have any doctors or lawyers in the family, but I had at least been to the doctor, so I decided that is what I would pursue. Between my sophomore and junior years of high school, my parents sent me to a week-long camp for aspiring doctors where I learned about college pre-med programs, medical school, and the different practice areas. It seemed interesting.

Then, I observed a surgery. I walked into the operating room as the procedure was already underway. The hiss of the surgeon's saw and the smell of singed skin filled the brightly lit room. I was standing in borrowed scrubs in the corner of the room, as far from the operating table as possible.

"Come on over and take a look," the doctor said. I inched forward.

"These are the vertebrae we are going to be fusing," the doctor said as he pointed with a scalpel into a gaping canyon in the patient's back while cold drops of sweat ran down mine.

"And this," the doctor said as he leaned forward and pointed deeper into the canyon, "is the spinal cord." I almost fainted, face first, into a man's open back. I did not stay for any of the procedure. I walked out to the hallway, sat with my back against the wall, and hugged my knees into my chest.

My aversion to surgery was not the only problem. By my junior year of high school, I found the math and science classes difficult. I was not failing, but I was far from being at the top of the classes, which I had learned at the doctor camp was important.

Meanwhile, I was developing a passion for writing, reading, and logic, which came easily to me and involved little to no cutting of flesh.

When it was time to pick a college, which was of course my only option, I chose a small liberal arts school in the town where my grandparents lived because they offered to cook dinner for me and do my laundry whenever I wanted. By my junior year of college, I was majoring in philosophy, English, and Spanish. So much for being a doctor or working in construction.

I NEEDED A plan to turn my education into a career. I had studied what I loved, and my collegiate education was phenomenal; I would put it up against anyone else's in the country. But I did not want to teach and did not know of any companies looking to hire a liberal arts triple major who had taken zero business classes and never opened Microsoft Excel.

During the winter of my junior year, I trimmed and bagged Christmas trees for people and considered moving north and becoming a lumberjack-poet combo. But I could not grow a full beard, so that was out.

The career counselor at my university had a different rec-ommendation. She looked at my transcript and then up at me.

"What do you like to do?" she asked.

"Read, write, and debate philosophy," I replied

"Have you considered law school?"

I sighed. My father was going to get his wish after all.

Within a few weeks of deciding to go to law school, I knew which school I was going to attend, which was presumptuous for someone who knew nothing about law schools. Not one person in my family or extended circle of friends was a lawyer. The only thing I knew was I had to take the Law School Admission Test (LSAT), and my GPA was competitive for the school I wanted to attend. I bought an LSAT study book and read it cover to cover over the weeks leading up to the test. The LSAT is a one-day speed exam. It is common for examinees to run out of time and guess for the last few questions in each section. Studying for and taking the LSAT was not fun. Many people take the LSAT two or three times in an attempt to improve their scores. When I walked out of the testing site, I knew I was not taking the test again, no matter what my score was.

I received the email with my score several weeks later while at a gas station on the way to tube the river with my friends. It was not bad, but it was not what I wanted. Maybe I could have scored a few points higher if I had taken one of the expensive prep courses or not spent as much time earlier that summer tubing the same river I was headed to at that moment. I was disappointed, but based on everything I had read, my combined GPA and LSAT score should have been enough to get me into the school I wanted to attend.

I secured my letters of recommendation from professors, prepared my personal statement, and sent my applications out to three schools: my dream school and two backups. Two weeks later, my dream school rejected me. No wait list, just a flat denial.

"They'll be sorry," I said. How exactly I was going to make a prestigious law school with a vast endowment sorry for not accepting me, I am not sure, but I was bitter.

Both of my backup schools accepted me, so it was decision time: University of Houston or Southern Methodist University? I spent a lot of time online comparing their programs, rankings, campuses, and reputations. They were neck and neck, but more of my friends were taking jobs in Houston, so that is where I chose to go. I visited the campus, bought a T-shirt, and found a few leads on apartments. I was ready to move and start the next chapter in my life—until my phone rang.

I worked as a waiter the summer after my senior year of college at the Italian food restaurant with the breadsticks. (You know which one I am talking about. And yes, I used to eat the breadsticks during my longer shifts.) One Friday, about halfway through summer, I was working a double, and my phone rang during my afternoon lunch break. The voice on the other end of the line introduced herself as an admissions representative from SMU.

"We were upset when we did not receive a commitment from you," she said. "We would like you to reconsider. One of our full-ride scholarships opened up this week, and we would like you to take it."

"A full ride as in a *full* ride?" I asked.

"Yes. It does not cover your living expenses, but it covers all tuition and fees," she said. I was shocked speechless. "Given how late we are in the admissions process, we cannot hold this scholarship open for long. If you would like to accept, you will have to do so by Monday."

"*This* Monday?" I asked.

"Yes," she answered.

I made the five-hour drive with my girlfriend the next day. We walked the campus and toured more than a dozen nearby budget apartments. I signed the admissions paperwork accepting the offer on Monday before I left to return home.

I STARTED LAW school just as blind as I had been during the admissions process. Other students knew about study outlines from prior years, how to lock in a low price for the bar exam study course three years early, and summer clerkships with a Big Law firm. From conversations with other students, I learned securing a summer clerkship with a Big Law firm for the summer between your second and third year was of the utmost importance.

"It's basically hopeless if you don't get one," my colleagues would say.

The Big Law firms interview students at the beginning of their second year, based on first-year grades. If you are not in the top 10 percent of your class, you should be concerned. If you are not in the top 25 percent of your class, you should not even bother applying. That was the message, loud and clear.

For the next year, I obsessed over securing a Big Law clerkship. I went to class, then read in the law library, then read at my apartment, then repeated. I took the bus from Dallas to San Antonio to visit my girlfriend on the weekends because I could not afford to lose five hours of study time driving each way. I also could not afford the gas to drive my pickup every weekend, but I would be able to afford it if I got a summer clerkship. More motivation.

There is only one grade given in each law school course: the final exam. You spend three months learning the material, but your grade is based entirely on the test you take in the final three hours. Final exams at the end of the first semester were a two-week blur of coffee and outlines, wrapped up and stretched to the tension of a bridge cable.

Some students showed up to the exams in the pajamas they had studied in all night, and others came wearing suits and ties in an effort to psych the other students out. I do not remember what I wore, but I did well on the exams. When the scores came out, I was well inside the top 10 percent of my class.

The second semester went the same, and I made the law school's flagship law review. I had put in the hard work and checked all the boxes for the clerkship resume. When I applied for the on-campus interviews the next fall, almost every Big Law firm gave me one of their fifteen-minute interview slots. I had more than twenty interviews in two weeks. I was ready to land a clerkship and start the next chapter of my life—until my phone did *not* ring.

The Big Law interview process has two steps. First, you have a fifteen-minute interview on campus. This is like speed dating for firms and students. A few attorneys from the firm spend all day on campus in small conference rooms in the career services office conducting back-to-back interviews. Then, the firms call the students they would like to interview again, this time at the firm's office. These call-back interviews last hours, as multiple attorneys from the firm interview the student.

I had no problem getting the fifteen-minute interviews. I bet I speed-dated more law firms than anyone else in the nation in 2013. My problem was that afterward, my phone did not ring. Not because it was broken, but because no one was calling it. I lugged my worthless, silent phone around for days, then weeks, and then months. Every time I got out of class, I pulled out my phone, desperate for a missed call. Nothing.

I congratulated all of my colleagues on law journal for landing clerkships with Big Law firms as I geared up for the second round of on-campus interviews, a process the other students in the top 10 percent knew nothing about.

The second round was with the medium-sized national firms and some regional firms. In the ultra-competitive law-student world, a clerkship with one of these firms was considered second class. I, however, did not have to worry about that stigma because the same nightmare played out—I got all of the fifteen-minute interviews, but zero callbacks.

By the midpoint of my third semester of law school, I had gone through more than fifty failed applications and interviews.

For the second time in three years, I found myself in a university career services office, off track from my plans and looking for a path. My career counselor set down my papers and looked at me.

"Have you thought about a boutique firm?" he asked.

"No," I answered.

"There is a book in the conference room next door that lists law firms by different boutique practice areas. Take a look and see if anything catches your eye. Just put it back on the shelf when you are done," he said.

I walked to the next room, opened the book, and started reading. Aviation. *Maybe.* Banking. *Not even close.* Construction. *Wait—what? There are law firms that focus on construction law?* I did not bother to read any further. I copied the names of all the construction firms and headed home to research.

One of the firms listed had an office in San Antonio, which was perfect, since my girlfriend had just received a full-time offer from a great company there. I had to email and call the firm multiple times over several weeks, but I got an interview. When my phone rang a few days after the interview, it was not for a callback; it was with an offer. I had a clerkship!

I do not know why I struck out on my first fifty interviews. Maybe my hair was too long; maybe I gave off too much lumberjack-poet vibe, or maybe God was guiding me to where He wanted me. After all of my worrying, I ended up at a firm that was a great fit for me.

As I write this, I still work for the same firm, practicing construction law. In my nine years of practice, I have learned something about construction: it never goes according to plan. Everything in construction revolves around the plans; they are what the architect draws and the contractor builds. But even in construction, where trained professionals spend months developing detailed plans, things happen, and the plans must change. Sometimes there is a mistake in the plans, sometimes there is an unforeseen condition at the project site, and sometimes things just get off schedule. Successful projects are the result not only of careful planning but also the ability to change plans.

Life is like a construction project in that regard. We need plans for our lives so that we will not wander aimlessly. But we have to remain flexible enough to change our plans. Things will happen that require change. Sometimes they are good, sometimes they are just different, and sometimes they are tragic.

Fear preys on our refusal to change plans. If we cannot change our plans, we will live in constant fear of all the things that might derail them. The best way I know to find peace in changing my plans is to trust in God's plans. I do not always know the details of God's plans, but I know they are for good and not for disaster, even in my darkest moments. I trust God sees the building He is making of me even when I cannot make sense of the plans on paper.

> FEAR PREYS ON OUR REFUSAL TO CHANGE PLANS.

GOD'S WORD ABOUT HIS PLANS FOR US:

✝ *"For I know the plans I have for you," says the* LORD. *"They are plans for good and not for disaster, to give you a future and a hope. In those days when you pray, I will listen. If you look for me wholeheartedly, you will find me.*

JEREMIAH 29:11–13 NLT

✝ *Then Job replied to the* LORD:

"I know that you can do all things;
no purpose of yours can be thwarted.
You asked, 'Who is this that obscures my plans without knowledge?'
Surely I spoke of things I did not understand,
things too wonderful for me to know."

JOB 42:1–3 NIV

✝ *Many are the plans in a person's heart, but it is the Lord's purpose that prevails.*

PROVERBS 19:21 NIV

Hey Pops —

Do you ever wish you could sleep as hard now as you did when you were a child? As children, we sleep so deeply that every morning is like a new life. But as we grow and take on more responsibilities, our sleep ebbs shallow and we wake in the night, worrying whether we paid a bill, sent an email, or missed a deadline. I remember some of the soundest nights of sleep for me were in the back seat of the car on Christmas Eve. We used to drive four hours from Seguin to Galveston in the middle of the night to split time with different parts of the family. As a child, I knew as long as you were driving I was safe. I think one year I even slept through a flat tire incident in which you had to unload all of the gifts from the back of the car to access the spare tire.

God wants us to live like children sleep. In Matthew 11:25-28, Jesus says God's truth is revealed to those who are "childlike," and instructs:

> Come to me, all of you who are
> weary and carry heavy burdens, and
> I will give you rest.

If we try to carry all of our burdens alone,

THE WEIGHT IS TOO HEAVY. WE MUST MAKE OURSELVES LIKE CHILDREN, WHO CAN REST IN RELIANCE ON THEIR PARENTS. JESUS DRIVES THIS POINT FURTHER IN LUKE 18:17, WHEN HE SAYS TO HIS DISCIPLES:

> TRULY I TELL YOU, ANYONE WHO WILL NOT RECEIVE THE KINGDOM OF GOD LIKE A LITTLE CHILD WILL NEVER ENTER IT.

AS YOU BATTLE THIS ILLNESS, DON'T FORGET TO REST IN CHRIST.

WE WILL FIGHT TOGETHER;
TOGETHER, WE WILL WIN.
WITH A SON'S LOVE FOR
HIS FATHER,

CHAPTER FOUR

Get Rest

Summer 2005 – League City, Texas

I FINISHED COUNTING BACKWARDS from fifty to zero. It did not work.

I tossed from my right side to my left and adjusted the covers. That did not work, either.

I opened my eyes and sat up on the edge of the bed for a minute. Then I got up and paced across the carpeted floor of my bedroom. I grabbed a guitar off the wall. I fidgeted with it for a minute, then put it back and resumed pacing.

I replayed the incident in my head over and over, amazed at the stupidity of what I had done. I looked over at my alarm clock; it was past 11:00 p.m. My dad had not scolded me when he got home that evening like I thought he would. I was glad for it at first, but this was worse. *He's going to punish me tomorrow or next week. He just wants me to lose sleep over it, then punish me,* I thought as I paced.

I KNEW IT was stupid as soon as I did it. It was a summer Saturday, and I was fifteen years old. I had spent a good chunk of the morning reading a book about surviving extreme situations. It talked about how to escape from quicksand, wrestle alligators, and kick down doors. I did not live in the wilderness or a war zone; I lived in a not-very-extreme south-Houston suburb. But I was a fifteen-year-old guy, and fifteen-year-old guys love that stuff. Actually, I still love that stuff.

I was thinking about that book as I mowed the lawn that afternoon. My parents were away for the day, and it was my job to do the yardwork. After that, I would have the rest of the day to do whatever I wanted. By the time I finished the last line of edging, energy was pulsing through my arteries. I had knocked out my task and was free for the rest of the day.

We kept the lawn tools in a detached garage. It had a big overhead door that we used for moving the riding lawnmower in and out, but it also had a standard door on the side that we used to access the smaller tools. I had already closed the big overhead door when I finished mowing and put the riding lawn mower away, so I stepped up to the side door. It was closed, and my hands were full—a weed eater in one and an edger in the other. *What a waste of time, to bend over, set the edger on the ground, stand back up, open the door with my hand, and then bend back over to pick up the edger again,* I thought. My mind replayed the instructions from the survival book: kick the keyhole of the deadbolt with your heel; this concentrates your maximum power on the critical point of the door.

Before I knew it, my leg was in motion. It lifted straight up, bent at the knee, and exploded forward. The heel of my shoe struck the keyhole of the deadbolt like a bullseye. It was the soundest contact I have ever made with a physical object, like when a Major League slugger connects the sweet spot of the bat to a fastball, and the ball screams out of the park. The door flew open. Splinters sprayed from the frame. The door remained connected at the hinges, but it was badly cracked. Worse yet, the side of the door frame opposite the hinges was destroyed. I stood motionless, still holding the tools, and closed my eyes. *That was stupid.*

I set the tools down and tried to close the door, but it no longer fit. The busted frame had lost its shape and collapsed inward. I could not get the door to close. *How am I going to explain this to my parents?* I thought. It is one thing to do something wrong with a comprehensible motive, like sneaking out past curfew or getting a speeding ticket. But this—I did not even know where to begin explaining this.

Would I tell my parents about the survival book I had been reading that morning? I could imagine the puzzled looks on their faces; they had no idea the book existed. Would I tell them about wanting to be more efficient at putting away the lawn tools? I could picture the anger on my father's face as he made me watch him set down and pick up the edger twenty times in the span of thirty seconds. There was no way to explain what I had done. No matter what I said, I knew what the response would be.

"What did you think would happen when you kicked the door? Did you think it would somehow open normally and you could close it back afterward?" my father would ask. "Do you know why there is a little knob on the door you can turn? So you can open the door without kicking it down," he might add.

I would not know how to respond because there would be no defense. I was going to have to sit there and listen to him tell me in a dozen different ways how dumb I had acted.

I put the weed eater and edger in the garage and pulled the door as closed as it would go. The sunny summer Saturday that moments ago had held so much freedom and hope now felt cold and gloomy. I had the rest of the day free, but could not enjoy it. I cleaned my room and vacuumed upstairs, trying to improve my overall resume for the day since there was nothing I could do about the busted door frame. When I was done with that, I paced around the house until my parents got home.

When they arrived, I asked them to follow me, walked over to the garage door, and showed them what I had done. I tried to explain my thought process a few times, but finally gave up and just stood there, waiting for the outburst. But nothing came. My father did not look angry. (He did not look happy, either.) He seemed to accept the situation so fast it looked almost as if he had already known about the door before I showed him. If my father said anything to me in the moment, it was so minor I do not remember it.

But I do remember the rest of the evening. At first, I was glad to get off easy. But as the evening wore on, I grew anxious. I could not sleep. *You did not get off easy; he's just thinking about some way to punish you*, I thought. I wished my parents had been angry. I wished they had screamed and sentenced me with a severe punishment. If I had the sentence, I could serve it and clear my name. If they had screamed really loudly, if in the heat of the moment they had said something nasty or sentenced me with a punishment too severe for the crime, then I might even have gotten a leg up out of the situation. I could have taken the unfair punishment and indebted my parents to me. But they had not, and I felt hopelessly in the wrong.

Sometime after 11:00 p.m., my father called me down from my room. I turned the corner at the base of the stairs and saw him standing in the kitchen.

"Sit down, son," he said. I looked at the kitchen bar. One of the barstools had before it a mountain of yellow sticky notes and a pen. I walked up to the barstool and sat down. My father did not sit.

"Grab one of the sticky notes," he said. I grabbed one of the little, square pads and peeled off the top note.

"Write your name on it." I grabbed the pen from the bar and wrote my name.

"Now, sign your name below that." I scribbled my signature across the note.

"Do that for all of the sticky notes." My eyes widened. I looked at the yellow tower before me, then back up at my father, but he was already walking to his home office. I grabbed the second sticky note and got started.

After an hour, I had an impressive stack of completed notes on my right-hand side, but the untouched notes on my left still towered over it. The wet sound of each sticky note being pulled from the next echoed in my head. The tips of my fingers had taken the shape of the pen. I thought about the nights I had seen my father working in the home office when I went to bed and again in the morning when I left for school. He could outlast me. I was playing his game, by his rules, on his turf. I stretched my neck to the right and left, then grabbed another sticky note, and then another, and then another.

When my father walked back into the kitchen, I finished the sticky note at hand and set the pen down. He looked at the stacks. I looked at the stacks. The completed tower and the untouched tower were about equal.

"You are fifteen years old, son," he said. "Next year, you are going to have a new level of freedom. You are going to be able to drive places on your own, and you are going to be responsible for more decisions. You did not think before you acted today. If you continue to act that way, you are going to have a life like this," he said and pointed to the sticky notes. "A life where you have to do the same, repetitive tasks over and over. I do not want you to have that life." He looked me in the eyes as he spoke. "You can go to bed. I love you."

My father never told me how stupid I was for kicking in the garage door. I had feared he would react with wrath and insult because that was how I felt about myself and what I had done. After my father got home, I feared he would not say anything and would leave me to suffer alone in my shame. I was in a Catch-22 of fear: afraid of the punishment that came with being guilty and afraid of the guilt that came from not being punished.

Fortunately, my father did not see the situation in the same myopic manner. He wanted me to know that what I had done was wrong—not so he could revel in the opportunity to punish me, but because he wanted me to be better. He knew my position was defenseless, but he also knew the more defenseless my position, the more likely I was to be defensive in response to ridicule. He neither punished me nor left me to suffer; he corrected me and forgave me.

I think God treats us like my father treated me that night. God created us with the free will to do as we choose. We, as a race of created beings, have chosen poorly through history. We have each, as individual created beings, chosen poorly at many points in our lives. There are consequences for these choices, like the busted door frame. But God does not revel in the opportunity to punish us or dismiss us to languish without Him. He chose a third option: He made the sacrifice to pay for the consequences of our choices. We are indebted to God, but the debt is forgiven. He does not ask us to do a certain number of good deeds; we cannot pay off the debt by cleaning our rooms or vacuuming the carpet. Instead, God asks us to accept His forgiveness by returning to Him and trying to live up to our God-given potential.

> WE DO NOT HAVE TO FEAR THE PUNISHMENT OF BEING GUILTY OR THE GUILT OF NOT BEING PUNISHED. GOD HAS A THIRD OPTION: MERCY.

I have made a lot of mistakes in my life. Some of them hurt other people instead of a door frame, and I have lost a lot of sleep because of them. Maybe you have, too, but that is not God's plan for us. We do not have to fear the punishment of being guilty or the guilt of not being punished. God has a third option: mercy. He wants us to realize our wrongdoing, accept His forgiveness, and rest in His mercy. God does not tell us how stupid we are when we kick in the garage door; He just says, "You can do better. I love you."

GOD'S WORD ABOUT MERCY AND REST:

✝ *Come to me, all you who are weary and burdened, and I will give you rest. Take my yoke upon you and learn from me, for I am gentle and humble in heart, and you will find rest for your souls.*

MATTHEW 11:28–29 NIV

✝ *This is what the Sovereign LORD, the Holy One of Israel, says:*

"In repentance and rest is your salvation,
in quietness and trust is your strength,
but you would have none of it.
You said, 'No, we will flee on horses.'
Therefore you will flee!
You said, 'We will ride off on swift horses.'
Therefore your pursuers will be swift!
A thousand will flee
at the threat of one;
at the threat of five
you will all flee away,
till you are left
like a flagstaff on a mountaintop,
like a banner on a hill."
Yet the LORD longs to be gracious to you;
therefore he will rise up to show you compassion.
For the LORD is a God of justice.
Blessed are all who wait for him!

ISAIAH 30:15–18 NIV

✝ *But when the kindness and love of God our Savior appeared, he saved us, not because of righteous things we had done, but because of his mercy. He saved us through the washing of rebirth and renewal by the Holy Spirit, whom he poured out on us generously through Jesus Christ our Savior, so that, having been justified by his grace, we might become heirs having the hope of eternal life.*

TITUS 3:4–7 NIV

Hey Pops —

I like when things are simple. Even when something is hard, it can still be simple. Take living on a budget as an example. If you spend less money than you make each month, you will save money. That may be hard, but at least it is simple.

Right now, you have a lot of complicated things in your life. The terminology of your illness, the chemistry behind your treatment, and the biology involved in your recovery. It is a blessing that God created talented people who can understand and work these complicated subjects to your advantage. But it is an even greater blessing that God has given you a simple tool: prayer.

Prayer is simple. We can pray to God from any place at any time. While there are eloquent and complex prayers, the best are often simple. For example, in James 5:13-15, the Bible says:

> Are any of you suffering hardships? You should pray. Are any of you happy? You should sing praises. Are any of you sick? You should call for the elders of the church to come and pray over you, annointing you with oil in the name of the Lord. Such a prayer offered in faith will heal the sick, and the Lord will make you well. And if you have committed any sins, you will be forgiven.

God makes it simple: if you are sick, pray. We don't have to partake in any complicated rituals or travel to a special place. Christ did the work and we just have to pray. But just because it is simple does not mean it is easy. We have to strengthen our faith and weaken our pride; we have to humble ourselves and admit we need God's help. I think this is one of the reasons God teaches us to pray with fellow believers. Every hardship we pray over is an opportunity not only to support the person in need but to strengthen our faith. Do not be afraid to ask for prayer; it is not a burden, but a blessing. And there are already more people praying for you than you think.

We will fight together;
together, we will win.
With a son's love for
his father,

CHAPTER FIVE

Stay Simple

Winter 2009 – League City, Texas

I LOOKED OVER MY right shoulder into the passenger seat. For the second time that morning, I watched a person climb into the car unaware of the mortal danger he was risking. This time, it was my Grandpa Tony, one of the most modest and gentle people I have ever known. He is a man of few words, and the few he speaks crawl out of his mouth in a mysterious accent somewhere between New Jerseyan and Cajun. He wears a ballcap, blue jeans, and Velcro tennis shoes every day, sporting a mustache he has not shaved since he got back from Vietnam in 1969. I looked at him as I searched for the clutch and started the car. I felt terrible for him.

I TOTALED MY first car during fall break of my freshman year of college in 2008. I was driving south down Highway

146 in my 2006 Dodge Charger, the car my father had bought me for my sixteenth birthday, before the housing market collapsed and his company went bankrupt. It was a sunny, clear morning. I had heavy metal on the radio, and my fingers were tapping along with the rhythm. I was headed to Galveston, but the driver of a silver Ford Mustang had other plans for me.

I was approaching one of those intersections where the highway traffic has flashing yellow lights and the smaller cross street has flashing red lights. When I was seconds from the intersection, a silver Ford Mustang lurched out from under the flashing red lights into the highway and stopped, longways across both of the southbound lanes. There was not enough time or room to brake. I glanced at the lanes left of the yellow line up ahead. There was no oncoming traffic. I veered left to pass around the front of the Mustang, but it lurched forward another fifteen feet and stopped. I braced for impact.

The airbag exploded into my face. I came to a stop on the opposing shoulder of the highway. A pungent white powder filled the air of my car. I undid my seat belt, opened the door, and stepped out. I turned around and looked back at the Mustang. The driver was out of the car and walking around. I exhaled. My passenger headlight had struck her driver headlight, barely avoiding a direct collision to her door. I took inventory of my body. The airbag had burnt a small patch on my left arm and bent my aviator sunglasses. Other than that, I was fine. My car was not. I did not need an insurance adjuster to tell me it was totaled.

I called my parents, and when they answered, I made sure to start with, "I'm okay." I rehearsed an, "It wasn't my fault" explanation as I waited for them on the side of the road, but I never had to use it. The positioning of the vehicles and the police report were enough for them. They just gave me a hug and took me to lunch.

I hitched a ride from family to get back to campus after Thanksgiving, then caught a ride with friends to come back home for Christmas break. By New Year's, I was ready to have a car again. My parents offered to replace the car, but our family's financial situation was different from what it had been two years prior. After my father's company went bankrupt, my parents were unable to keep up with the payments on their house (the one where I kicked in the garage door) and lost it in foreclosure. In response, my father did what he always did: worked hard and found another way to provide for his family.

He took a job with a different new-home company in Georgia, where he lived alone, except for the four nights per week that his new employee slept on the couch. My mother stayed behind in Texas and moved into an apartment across town from our old house so my brother could continue his education in the same school system.

Our family found a way to make it work, but a 2006 Dodge Charger was not in the budget. That was fine with me. I did not want the same car. I had my heart set on something else.

"What kind of car are you thinking about?" my mother asked.

"I want a stick shift," I answered. "Nothing fancy—just a cheap, simple stick shift."

She looked at me. "Do you know how to drive a stick shift?" she asked.

"Yes, I practiced last year." I did not mention the practice was thirty minutes one afternoon, during which I stalled a half-dozen times for each successful start. I did not care. I was eighteen years old, and I wanted a stick-shift car. Nothing with an automatic transmission was going to be acceptable, and anything with a stick shift would do.

"Okay, let's look tomorrow," she said.

My Grandpa Tony came with us to the local car lot the next day to cosign on the purchase. We found a great deal on a Toyota Corolla with manual locks, manual windows, and, of course, a manual transmission. I was sold.

"Do you want to take it for a test drive?" the salesman offered.

"No, I'm —"

"Yes, he'll take it for a test drive," my mother interrupted before I could finish.

My heart raced as the salesman handed me the key. I opened the door, sat down, and slid the key into the ignition; the salesman sat in the passenger seat. I leaned back and looked down at the pedals. I identified the clutch by process of elimination and pushed it with my left foot while I checked to make sure the stick was in neutral. I remembered that much. I turned the key and started the engine.

The salesman started telling me about the safety features and the car's tremendous reliability. I wanted to tell him the car was already sold; it had a stick shift, and we were going to buy it. I wanted to tell him he should save his breath so he could hold it once I started driving.

But I did not say anything. I just put the stick in first gear, laid on the gas far beyond necessary, and eased off the clutch like a sloth. I was not going to stall out in front of the salesman. The engine revved like a jet until the car jerked into gear; we were off. The salesman lost his words for a second, then carried on with his pitch as if nothing had happened, but I saw him shift in his seat and grab the armrest on the door. At every gear change the engine revved and the car jolted, but three minutes later we made it back to the lot without incident. I think the salesman directed me along the shortest test-drive route he knew, which worked for me. I wanted to be in the car alone so I could practice without shame.

When we signed the paperwork, I was ecstatic. I owned a stick shift! As we walked out of the building and into the parking lot, my mother turned to me.

"Would you drive your grandpa back to his house in your new car?" my mother asked. "I have some errands to run."

I went cold. I had not accounted for this move. From the dealership, it was a thirty-mile drive to my grandfather's house in Galveston down a busy interstate. But what could I say now? That I did not really know how to drive the car I had just watched my mother buy me? No. Instead, I sat silently as I watched my grandfather buckle into the passenger seat and put his life into my inexperienced hands.

I looked down at the stick and pushed it up into first gear. Then, I looked at the tachometer, the gauge that measures the number of RPMs the engine is doing. I had never paid attention to it when I was driving an automatic, but I was told it was important for driving a stick shift. I knew I was supposed to shift gears when the tachometer was somewhere between two thousand and three thousand. But I was also told I should shift gears based on the sound the engine was making. It was a lot to think about. I had to work the clutch with my left foot, work the gas and brake pedals with my right foot, control the stick with my right hand, steer the car with my left hand, watch the tachometer along with the road, and listen to the sounds the engine was making, all at the same time. God forbid I should need to signal for a turn.

I pushed the gas, watched the tachometer, backed off the clutch, and rolled into first gear with only a slight hiccup. I was impressed with myself as I navigated the lot and pulled up to the exit onto the feeder road. I stopped with the clutch engaged and the stick in first. I looked left. There was a steady stream of traffic—not enough to slow the cars down, but too much to allow for a long gap to form. The clutch felt heavy under my leg. A short gap opened up, and then another, but I did not turn onto the road.

I waited through at least ten gaps I would have turned into with an automatic transmission. There was no sign a larger gap would open, and I could not sit at the exit all day. I picked a car. When it passed, I pushed on the gas and eased off the clutch, but the car did not come into gear. I panicked and thought I was letting off the clutch too slow, so I snapped my leg back and released it. The car jerked forward onto the feeder road, then stopped. I had stalled. I was sitting diagonal across a lane of traffic with a fifty-miles-per-hour speed limit.

A horn blared and tires squealed around me. The car at the other end of the gap I tried to shoot swerved around my car. More traffic was coming. *Come on, come on, come on,* I thought as I turned the keys to the off position in the ignition and restarted the process. I pushed the clutch in, started the car, floored the gas, and shot out into first gear. I pulled into second, then third, then fourth, and was up to speed with the rest of traffic.

I said nothing to my grandfather as I merged onto the interstate, and he said nothing to me, so I can only imagine what was going through his mind. The ride smoothed out once I got into fifth gear on the highway, but I was worried. I knew what lay ahead.

When you cross the causeway into Galveston, you enter a grid of four-way intersections. The interstate becomes Broadway, and there are nine stoplights in the thirty city blocks between the edge of town and Grandpa Tony's street. The lights are timed: if you hit the first light on green, you will sail through the rest; if you hit the first light on red, you are in for a stop-and-start drive.

We crested the causeway, passed Offatts Bayou, and crossed over 61st Street. The light was red. I came to a stop and shifted into neutral. Nine times. I was going to have to start nine times with Grandpa Tony in the car.

I looked at the tachometer, got ready to repeat the process, and waited for the light to turn green.

"Push the gas and let off the clutch at the same time, like you're changing one for the other," Grandpa Tony suggested.

I looked over at him, stunned. I had never heard him give anyone advice before. I had not heard him say much of anything other than one-line jokes, stories about the 1950s and old movies, and lamentations about the dismal state of the Dallas Cowboys in the post-Troy Aikman era. I looked back ahead at the red light. It turned green, and I followed his instructions. I did not stall, but it was far from smooth. We pulled up to the next red light.

"Just go real easy on the clutch until you feel it catch, then let it go," Grandpa Tony said. The light turned green, and we rolled out without a hitch.

"There we go, jack!" Grandpa Tony said. I made it through all of the remaining intersections without stalling.

THE HARDEST PART of learning to drive a stick shift is getting the car moving. If you can get it into first gear, the car's momentum makes cruising down the highway easy. But when you are starting from a cold stop, you have to supply the momentum. The start can be explained in complicated terms, with RPMs and engine sounds, but I found the best approach in the simple advice I received from my grandfather.

For me, learning to pray was a lot like learning to drive a stick shift. As a child, I prayed the typical nursery-rhyme style prayers. But as an adult and former atheist just starting to believe in God and the resurrection of Jesus Christ, praying, "Now I lay me down to sleep" like I had when I was eight years old seemed inadequate. I wanted to pray to God with my own words, but I did not know how.

My prayer car was at a cold stop; it had no momentum. To get it moving, I had to do multiple things at once, just like driving a stick shift. I had to recognize God's primacy, humble myself, submit to His will, and operate with faith, even though I had doubts. When I was learning to pray, I stalled out a lot, usually for two reasons.

Sometimes, I was too slow on the gas. I had doubts, which caused me to hold back rather than committing to the prayer. But you cannot get a car into first gear or a prayer off the ground without committing to the gas pedal. Other times, I was too preoccupied with making a complicated and perfect prayer. I got caught up in trying to feel a certain emotion or achieve a particular mental focus on God, so I stalled out before I ever started.

Since then, I learned prayer does not have to be complicated. My favorite prayer is only four words long: "Thy will be done." It is simple, but it is powerful. Simple prayers provide courage on complicated days. When we are hurting, sick, or gripped by fear, it is hard to think. Our minds seem to race to no destination. Reciting a twenty-verse prayer and achieving a state of tranquil meditation might not be possible when we have just found out our house burned down or our child is being rushed to the hospital.

> SIMPLE PRAYERS PROVIDE COURAGE ON COMPLICATED DAYS.

The good news is God does not want us to make it complicated. He tells us we should pray. And if things are really hard, we should ask others to pray with us. God wants us to keep it simple.

GOD'S WORD ABOUT PRAYER:

✝ *Are any of you suffering hardships? You should pray. Are any of you happy? You should sing praises. Are any of you sick? You should call for the elders of the church to come and pray over you, anointing you with oil in the name of the Lord. Such a prayer offered in faith will heal the sick, and the Lord will make you well. And if you have committed any sins, you will be forgiven.*

JAMES 5:13–15 NLT

✝ *This, then, is how you should pray:*
"Our Father in heaven,
hallowed be your name,
your kingdom come,
your will be done,
on earth as it is in heaven.
Give us today our daily bread.
And forgive us our debts,
as we also have forgiven our debtors.
And lead us not into temptation,
 but deliver us from the evil one."

MATTHEW 6:9–13 NIV

✝ *Hear my prayer, LORD;*
   let my cry for help come to you.
Do not hide your face from me
   when I am in distress.
Turn your ear to me;
   when I call, answer me quickly. . . .
For the LORD will rebuild Zion
   and appear in his glory.
He will respond to the prayer of the destitute;
   he will not despise their plea.

PSALMS 102:1–2,16–17 NIV

Hey Pops—

Some people respond to the bad things in their lives with denial or wishful thinking. I suppose if we had no hope, denial and wishful thinking would be our best options. But we do have hope. We have hope that God will help and heal us in this mortal life and greater hope that through faith in Christ we will be raised forever.

This is why denial and wishful thinking are dangerous. If we build a shelter on the sands of denial and wishful thinking, we will never find the solid rock of God's word. If we don't confront evil, we will miss our weapon provided to conquer it. In Genesis 1, when God created the world, he repeatedly looked upon creation and "saw that it was good ... that it was very good!" This illness you are battling was not a part of God's creation. It, like all other evil, is the product of sin, first committed by Satan when he rebelled against God, replicated by Adam and Eve when Satan deceived them, and repeated by humanity throughout the generations.

The enemy will seek to use this illness to steal, kill, and destroy, not your mortal body, but your hope in Christ. Tell the enemy, "Not today. Today is not the day I give in to despair. Today is not the day I curse God for misfortune. Today is not the

DAY I HARDEN MY HEART IN RESENT. TODAY
IS NOT THE DAY I START TO LOVE OTHERS
LESS. TODAY IS NOT THE DAY I LOSE HOPE.
NOT TODAY."
STAY VIGILANT AND KEEP THIS SPIRIT OF HOPE
EVERYDAY. WE ARE CALLED NOT TO HIDE FROM
EVIL BUT TO OVERCOME IT.

WE WILL FIGHT TOGETHER;
TOGETHER, WE WILL WIN.
WITH A SON'S LOVE FOR
HIS FATHER,

CHAPTER SIX

Bounce Back

June 28, 2020 – Gillespie County, Texas

I HEARD A CRASH and then a cry of pain I will never forget. I unclipped from my pedals, threw my bike in the grass, and ran down the hill. I saw him lying on his back in the shallow water. "Call 911!" I shouted to his wife. I walked out to him as the water flowed around my bike cleats. *This can't be happening*, I thought. But it was. I sat in the water next to him and put my hand on his shoulder as we waited for the ambulance.

MY WIFE, HANNAH, and I were born within three weeks of each other, so we share a birthday season each year. When we were turning thirty, we decided to do something big. I signed up to run fifty miles (more on that later), and we both signed up for a Half Ironman triathlon in Lubbock, Texas.

These were ambitious goals. I was a mediocre sprinter and powerlifter in high school. The 800-meter run, two laps around the track, was long distance for most of my life. My longest run was a miserable half-marathon, at the end of which I promptly lost everything I had eaten that day. Hannah is a natural athlete, the kind of person who can play any sport better than average, but she had never done any sort of endurance training. We hired a coach and started training on February 1, 2020, for the June 28, 2020, race.

One month later, COVID-19 hit. Organized races around the world were being canceled, but the Lubbock triathlon was still on the calendar. When we were one month away, it started to feel real. When we were one week away, the race was still set, all systems go.

The weekend before the race, Hannah and I did a miniature practice triathlon with our coach and a few of the other athletes she was training. That is where I met Rick, who was also registered to compete in Lubbock.

The first thing I noticed about Rick, as we waded into the water to start our training swim, was the word "JESUS" tattooed in huge letters across his stomach. The second thing I noticed was him encouraging everyone else in the water. I liked him immediately. He was a fifty-something-year-old cancer survivor who had completed numerous triathlons, including a full Ironman. He had failed to reach the finish line at only one triathlon in his life: Lubbock. And he was ready for redemption.

On race week, our energy magnified with each passing day. The Lubbock Half Ironman was going to be the first organized race in months, maybe anywhere in the United States or even world. Hannah and I had bib numbers, check-in times, and a pantry full of race food. We had race plans, packing lists, and two days off work. We were ready. And then, three days before the race, we got the email: It was canceled. After months of training, we were like archers with arrows notched and elbows drawn back. We had tremendous energy built up, waiting to be unleashed, but the target had vanished.

Within two hours of the cancellation, I had a new personal triathlon mapped out for us in the Texas Hill Country, about an hour away from our home in San Antonio. We had worked too hard to lounge by the pool that weekend.

The swim was easy to plan. We had trained in the Guadalupe River two weekends prior and knew a great out-and-back route from a public boat ramp. There were also trails alongside the river, so there was no difficulty in planning the run.

But the bike portion was different. Planning a fifty-six-mile, race-day-quality bike course without the benefit of road closures is tough. First, it has to be safe. The faster the traffic on the roads typically is, the wider the shoulder needs to be. Second, it has to have as few interruptions as possible. This was supposed to be a real race; stopping at dozens of traffic lights would ruin the vibe.

After three attempts, I found a route I liked. We would head out from Kerrville on Highway 16 to Fredericksburg, make a sharp left and ride a fifteen-mile loop on back roads, and then merge back onto Highway 16 to return. It had twice the elevation gain we had been training for, but it would have to do. You cannot avoid hills while building a fifty-six-mile cycling route through the Texas Hill Country. I tried.

I named our new race the Kerrville COVID Crusher 70.3. Two days before the big day, I invited Rick to join us.

I knew how ready he was for the Lubbock race and how disappointed he had been about the cancellation. The day before the race, Hannah and I headed up to Kerrville. We picked up my buddy, Davey J, who was doing the race with us and met Rick at the public boat ramp to pre-drive the bike course. The traffic on Highway 16 would be fast, but we had a wide shoulder. And while there were no shoulders on the back road loop, there was very little traffic.

Everything looked good until we came to a water crossing at mile forty, just before we would be merging back onto Highway 16. The back road narrowed to a one-lane crossing of the Pedernales River. Instead of a bridge, the road dipped down into the river, and about one inch of water flowed over the top of it. I drove across slowly, looking out the open window at the water. When we reached the other side, I pulled over. Rick pulled up next to me.

"What do you think?" I asked.

"It will be fine. I've gone through worse," he replied.

"Sounds good," I said, and rolled the window up.

I woke up the next morning at 4:45 a.m. It was raining. I watched the water come down as I drank my coffee and worried about the crossing. When we got to the swim start, I told everyone my concern. Davey J pointed out it had not rained that far north.

"If we get there and the water is too high, we'll just unclip and walk our bikes across," Rick said.

"Okay, I like that plan," I said.

The rain stopped just before we started the swim. I said a few words to commemorate our makeshift race, reminded everyone where the aid vehicles would be parked, and gave one last warning about the river crossing. Then, I counted us down: "Five, four, three, two, one!"

We pushed off into the swim to the sound of applause from a small but passionate crowd: Rick's wife; Davey J's father; and Davey J's wife, AJ, who kayaked in front of us to help with sighting.

After the swim, we peeled our wetsuits off and hopped on our bikes. We started the ride as a foursome, but by mile two Rick had pulled ahead, and I noticed Davey J had dropped off. I pulled over and called him.

"I got a dang flat. Y'all keep going," he said.

Hannah and I clipped back in and pedaled forward. The route felt like it was all ups and downs with no flats, but we made good time to the first makeshift aid station around mile twenty-five. When we pulled up, we refueled and refilled our supplies.

"How far ahead is Rick?" I asked.

"About ten minutes ahead of you," AJ said. Hannah and I clipped back in and headed out.

The next stretch of the route had a rough crosswind as we climbed up and down more hills. It was tough, but we pushed through with a decent pace and turned back toward Highway 16. I was surprised when we caught up to Rick just before the river crossing at mile forty. I pulled ahead, and Rick filed in behind Hannah.

As we approached the river, I wrapped my fingers over the brakes and prepared to stop, but the water height and flow looked the same as the day before. I picked a line and glided across without a problem. I glanced in the rearview mirror attached to my helmet and watched Hannah follow my line, no problems. I made the ninety-degree right turn and started to climb the hill. Then, I heard it: a crash followed by a cry of pain.

I unclipped, threw my bike over, and sprinted down the hill in the grass. I turned the corner and saw Rick lying on his back in the water. His right foot was pointing in the wrong direction. I shouted at his wife in the support vehicle to call 911 as I heel-walked through the water in my cleats. I sat down next to him. He was in serious pain, the kind most people go all of their life without experiencing. I wished Davey J, a flight nurse who saves people for a living, was there instead of me. What could I do to help Rick? "You can be a doctor or a lawyer," my father had told me. The other choice would have been more useful at this point.

I put my hand on Rick's shoulder and watched the water flow around us. He stopped shouting. For a second, the only sounds around us were the trickling water and Rick's labored breathing. Then, I heard a soft voice. Rick started whispering one word over and over: "Jesus."

That is all he said, nothing else but "Jesus." I knew he wanted to say words he could not find, so I prayed with him. I prayed for God to take the pain away and to give him peace and rest. I prayed for God to bless the paramedics and doctors with wisdom and skill to heal his injuries.

It was not eloquent, and I did not quote verses. I kept it simple and prayed as best as I could in the moment, and when I finished, Rick prayed, "Your will be done." Then, he looked up at me and asked if his bike was damaged. I told him it looked fine as far as I could see. He looked relieved and did something that blew me away. Lying in the water with his foot pointing in the wrong direction, he told me how hard he was going to work on rehab and which race he would do next. His leg had been broken for less than ten minutes.

In an instant, Rick had experienced shock, severe physical pain, immense disappointment that he would not finish the race, and the dread of knowing how hard he would have to train to rehab his leg. But he had quickly overcome all of that and started looking forward. He was not sorry for himself or angry about his misfortune. He put his trust in God and found peace in less than ten minutes.

It took me a long time to learn that God does not promise us a life free of hardships and pain. I struggled to make sense of why bad things happen to people who are trying to do good.

> GOD NEVER PROMISED US A FAIR LIFE

As a philosophy and law student, reality seemed unfair and inconsistent with the possibility of there being an all-good god. But I later learned God never promised us a fair life. Fairness is a human concept we created in response to the presence of evil. Jesus talked a lot about love and forgiveness, but He mentioned fairness only once as far as we know, and that was to show us our human expectation of fairness is not applicable to the Kingdom of God (Matthew 20: 1-16). It was not fair for Jesus, who had no blame, to be sacrificed for us, who had blame. It was an act of love, forgiveness, and justice, but it was not fair. It was the most unfair event in the history of the world. And yet, it was the greatest triumph of good over evil.

Fear does not fight fairly; it loves to use unfair things to its advantage. A serial killer who murders random victims is scarier than someone who kills an ex-lover. A brain tumor of unknown origin is scarier than lung cancer after forty years of smoking two packs a day. When we expect a cause-and-effect relationship and cannot see one, fear moves in. Fear tells us unfair things can happen to anyone at any time, so we should constantly worry. It is a powerful move, but there is an antidote: We can stop obsessing over the unfairness of our challenges and focus on overcoming them. We take the sting of fear from potential blows by handling the ones we actually receive.

What happened to Rick during the race was not fair, but it happened. Rick got five screws and a plate put in his leg that afternoon while the rest of us pressed on to finish the race. When Rick was lying on his back in an inch of the Pedernales River with his foot pointing the wrong direction, he could have seen it as a tragic ending to a storyline in his life, but he did not. He saw it as the starting line for his new race.

Within one week, Rick signed up for another triathlon. His perspective paid off. Less than ten months after breaking his leg, he crossed the finish line of his next Half Ironman. I want to face my challenges in life the way Rick did in the river that day: big on trust in God and light on self-pity. I want to see every bad blow as an opportunity to defeat fear and shine in God's glory.

GOD'S WORD ABOUT HARDSHIP AND PERSEVERANCE:

✝ *Consider it pure joy, my brothers and sisters, whenever you face trials of many kinds, because you know that the testing of your faith produces perseverance. Let perseverance finish its work so that you may be mature and complete, not lacking anything.*

JAMES 1:2–4 NIV

✝ *But Joseph said to them, "Don't be afraid. Am I in the place of God? You intended to harm me, but God intended it for good to accomplish what is now being done, the saving of many lives."*

GENESIS 50:19–20 NIV

✝ *The Lord will rescue me from every evil attack and will bring me safely to his heavenly kingdom. To him be glory for ever and ever. Amen.*

2 TIMOTHY 4:18 NIV

Hey Pops —

Have you ever seen those little yellow books called CliffsNotes at a book store? They provide summaries of classic literary works. If you read the summary of, for example, Shakespeare's _A Midsummer Night's Dream_, you will know the plot of the play. But you will not have experienced what makes this play a work of art.

I think our lives are the same way. If we read a summary of the plot of someone's life, we will know generally where the person came from and what he did in life. But we do not know what makes a person great until we learn the details — the anecdotes from close friends and family — or, better yet, meet him.

God gave us the opportunity to do just that. In John 1:14, the apostle John wrote:

> The Word became flesh and made his dwelling among us. We have seen his glory, the glory of the one and only Son, who came from the Father, full of grace and truth.

We do not have a mere summary of God's creation of the world and plan. We have seen him. The Son became human and lived

A HUMAN LIFE BEFORE WITNESSES. WHEN JESUS DIED AND THEN DEFEATED DEATH, THOSE WITNESSES RECORDED JESUS' HUMAN LIFE. GOD, LIKE A GOOD FATHER, WANTED HIS CHILDREN NOT ONLY TO RECEIVE INSTRUCTIONS, BUT TO KNOW HIM. WE SHOULD STRIVE EACH DAY TO KNOW HIM MORE.

WE WILL FIGHT TOGETHER;
TOGETHER, WE WILL WIN.
WITH A SON'S LOVE FOR
HIS FATHER,

CHAPTER SEVEN

Come See

December 31, 2018 – Na Pali Coast, Kauai

I LOOKED OUT ACROSS the water at the green ridges that climbed to the sky and the valleys between them. It was as if all the beauty of Earth erupted from the middle of the ocean. I was speechless as the boat rocked on the rolling waves. *I was wrong*, I thought. *So wrong.*

AT THE END of every year, Hannah and I travel somewhere with our friends Sarah and Chad to celebrate the New Year. On the flight home, each of us writes a destination on a small piece of paper, folds the paper in half, and throws it into my hat. Then, one of us scrambles the papers, draws one, and announces where we are going for the next New Year.

Several years ago, we spent the New Year in Paris during an unusually cold spell, and I loved it! The city felt electric as the Eiffel Tower sparkled in the crisp air. Our hotel rooms were tiny, but there was a ledge outside our windows with a view of Notre Dame.

Hannah, on the other hand, did not love it. She walked the streets of Paris as a bundle of scarves and jackets and claims she did not warm up until two weeks after we got back home to Texas. She was very glad on the flight home to learn we were going to New Orleans for the next New Year.

One year later, when we arrived in New Orleans, a harsh cold front blew in. The temperature dropped into the twenties while the humidity stayed above 60 percent. I have never felt air so humid be so cold. It soaked through our clothes and chilled our bones. And I loved it, again.

Hannah walked the streets of New Orleans an even fluffier bundle than in Paris. When we got on the plane to head home, she was determined to spend the next New Year somewhere, anywhere, guaranteed to be warm. When we drew the winning paper from my hat, it was hers. We were going to Hawaii.

Hannah and I had never talked about going to Hawaii, so her choice caught me by surprise. *New Year's Eve is meant to be spent in a city, with culture and celebrations*, I thought. *Not on an island.* Scenes from movies of tourist-trap luaus and families in matching Hawaiian shirts played through my head. I wanted to travel somewhere unique and vibrant, not to America's overly commercialized playground.

As the winner of the drawing, Hannah got to plan the details of the trip. Her first order of business was picking which island we would visit. After consulting with the group, she selected Kauai.

When we landed on the small island, we rented a Jeep and settled in. We started the day on New Year's Eve with a boat tour of the Na Pali coast. We arrived at Kikiaola Harbor on the south side of the island half an hour before our scheduled 9:00 a.m. departure. "Harbor" is a generous word for what the place actually is, with its crooked wooden dock, one boat ramp, and two picnic tables. There were about fifty people competing for shade under the lone canopy. We joined the group and waited.

After a few minutes, a pickup pulled up and launched a boat into the water. The captain backed the boat away from the ramp while two deckhands jumped from the truck and helped him tie to the dock. After calling the roster of passengers for this boat (not us), the two deckhands escorted them aboard, untied from the dock, and pushed away. The coordination of the captain and his crew impressed me; they moved like the pieces of a clock.

Our boat arrived a few minutes later when another pickup pulled into the harbor. The pickup launched the boat into the water, and the captain backed the boat away from the ramp, just like the first. But then the pickup drove off.

I looked around to see if the deckhands had come by a different vehicle, but there was no one. I turned back to look at our boat. The captain was a shirtless, middle-aged man with shaggy, dirty-blonde hair. He pulled the boat up alongside the dock and tossed two ropes onto the wood. The boat was still moving forward at a good clip, parallel to the dock, when he jumped. As soon as his leather flip-flop hit the dock, his foot shot out from under him. He fell square on his butt, then scrambled up and chased the ropes slithering along the dock behind the boat.

"Oh great, we got Captain Ron," I said to Hannah. Our captain grabbed one of the ropes and tied the boat off just before he ran out of dock.

We climbed aboard with him. As it turned out, he did have a deckhand; the guy who was driving the pickup joined us just before we headed out. From the harbor, we followed the coastline around the island. As we headed north, our captain pulled over to an archway in the cliff. The jagged rock face turned pink and opened to reveal a hidden chamber. The water rose and fell as the ocean breathed in and out of the arch.

Through the cave, we could see an opening where the sun poured in and highlighted a single rock jutting out from the ocean, perfectly centered in the round chamber. The captain turned the back of the boat toward the cave opening, then put it in reverse.

Oh no, I thought as he backed into the cave. *He's going to try to thread the needle.*

We rose and fell with the swell of the ocean as we squeezed into the tight passage. The rock walls of the cave were just feet away from us on either side, but our captain was unfazed. He backed us through the narrow tunnel and into the sun-bathed chamber. The whir of the wind faded away, and the captain cut the engine.

No one spoke. The only sound was the water lapping on the bright pink rocks around us. It was a place you might stay for only a moment but never forget. Our captain cut the engine on, waited for the water to hit the perfect level, then pushed the throttle down and shot back out through the cave in the finest bit of boat piloting I have ever seen.

The cave was just a preview of the beauty to come. As we continued north, the Na Pali Coast revealed a view unlike anything I had ever seen. The land erupted from the sea to the sky in sharp ridges with valleys between them. The red dirt and green vegetation of the land stood in sharp contrast to the deep blue Pacific Ocean.

I stared, captivated. I thought about the vast ocean behind me. It was more than three thousand miles to the next land mass. These magnificent cliffs were at the edge of the map—the western face of this western island. They were the last thing the setting sun bathed in light each day.

I was still in awe when it was time to head back to the harbor. We had soaked up every second possible and were behind schedule for our return, so Captain Ron opened the engines up to full throttle. We bounced across the rolling waves and sprayed the sea in our wake. I sat in the back with my arm around Hannah, dazed by the beauty I had experienced over the last four hours.

And then, he did it. Captain Ron played Israel "IZ" Kamakawiwo'ole's version of "Somewhere Over the Rainbow" on the boat's speakers. It did not feel cheesy or clichéd. The song had never sounded so beautiful to me, as if all the times I heard it before were through a muffled speaker. The perfection of the moment was overwhelming.

As it turns out, Kauai—the place I did not want to go—ended up becoming my favorite place in the world. I thought I knew what Hawaii was going to be like from what I had read and heard, but no secondhand information could prepare me for what it was like to actually be there.

I EXPERIENCED SOMETHING similar with my faith. As a kid, I learned just enough about Christianity to think I knew what it was. I went to church occasionally and even got baptized during my freshman year of high school. But my understanding of faith was superficial. This was in part because I was young and fortunate enough to live a relatively healthy and tragedy-free life up through my graduation from high school. More importantly, though, I had not experienced faith because I had not lived in it. I was an outsider even as an insider.

My superficial understanding of Christianity did not hold up for long. The more I studied in college, the more cynical I became about it. It was a childish religion, full of impossibly simple accounts of creation, which Christians then defended with impossibly complicated explanations. It was built on and spread through emotions, which is why I had fallen for it at age fourteen. And any rational person could see Christianity was hollow because half of the people who went to church every Sunday were rude snobs Monday through Saturday. It was a social club—maybe an important one to be a member of, but I was not the sort of person who could ignore my intelligence and pretend to believe in such things.

There was a problem with this thought process. The problem was not my college education, which increased my critical thinking ability and made my life richer. The problem was that I was critiquing something I thought I understood but did not. When I experienced real Christianity for the first time—a journey I will share in the next two chapters—I realized it is not something abstract to be pondered; it is something personal to be lived. I am not saying Christianity is subjective; it has truth claims that are either objectively true or false. But Christianity is, at its core, personal.

It is the story of a personal God who created people, then became a human person to save those people. It is the best explanation I know for our overwhelming sense of personhood—the feeling that each of us is a unique and valuable person—and it is the most beautiful story I have ever heard. But it is not just a story we are told; it is a story in which we are invited to participate.

> CHRISTIANITY IS NOT A POSTCARD WE ARE SENT, BUT A PLACE TO WHICH WE ARE INVITED.

No amount of learning about Christianity from the outside can teach a person what it is really about, just as no amount of hearing about Kauai can prepare a person for the beauty of standing on a boat before the towering Na Pali Coast. Christianity is not a postcard we are sent, but a place to which we are invited. We must accept that invitation in order to experience the type of life-changing faith that is capable of conquering fear.

GOD'S WORD ABOUT BEING WITH US:

✝ *The word became flesh and made His dwelling among us. We have seen his glory, the glory of the one and only Son, who came from the Father, full of grace and truth.*

JOHN 1:14 NIV

✝ *As Jesus walked beside the Sea of Galilee, he saw Simon and his brother Andrew casting a net into the lake, for they were fishermen. "Come, follow me," Jesus said, "and I will send you out to fish for people." At once they left their nets and followed him.*

When he had gone a little farther, he saw James son of Zebedee and his brother John in a boat, preparing their nets. Without delay he called them, and they left their father Zebedee in the boat with the hired men and followed him.

MARK 1:16–20 NIV

✝ *Now Thomas (also known as Didymus), one of the Twelve, was not with the disciples when Jesus came. So the other disciples told him, "We have seen the Lord!"*

But he said to them, "Unless I see the nail marks in his hands and put my finger where the nails were, and put my hand into his side, I will not believe."

A week later his disciples were in the house again, and Thomas was with them. Though the doors were locked, Jesus came and stood among them and said, "Peace be with you!" Then he said to Thomas, "Put your finger here; see my hands. Reach out your hand and put it into my side. Stop doubting and believe."

Thomas said to him, "My Lord and my God!"

Then Jesus told him, "Because you have seen me, you have believed; blessed are those who have not seen and yet have believed."

JOHN 20:24–30 NIV

Hey Pops —

I used to think prayer was a selfish, hypocritical practice. I imagined people praying were like bratty children pestering their parents for ice cream and new toys. I had this misguided conception because some people really do pray this way and I assumed all people prayed similarly.

My conception of prayer changed when I read what the Bible actually says about prayer. When we pray according to the Bible, we are not like bratty children asking for more indulgences, but humble children asking our parents for help. While I am not yet a father, I think all good parents encourage their children to ask for help when they need it, especially if it is help to ~~become the~~ grow into the people the children are meant to be.

This is the type of prayer the Bible teaches. In Mark 9:23-25, Jesus tells the father of a sick child that "all things are possible to him who believes." In response, the father "cried out and said with tears,

'Lord I believe; help my unbelief.'"

This was one of the most important verses in my conversion from an atheist back to a Christian. The father's declaration is six words long. In the first three he says he

BELIEVES, BUT IN THE SECOND THREE HE SAYS HE DOES NOT BELIEVE. THIS VERSE WOULD BE AN INCONSISTENT RIDDLE, BUT FOR THE WORD "HELP." THE FATHER ASKS JESUS TO "HELP MY UNBELIEF." THIS FLOORED ME THE FIRST TIME I REALIZED WHAT IT MEANT. WE CAN, EVEN AS SKEPTICS, PRAY TO GOD TO HELP WITH OUR DOUBTS. WE DO NOT HAVE TO BE 100%, 90%, OR EVEN 51% CERTAIN IN GOD'S TRUTH TO PRAY. AS LONG AS WE HAVE THE 1% OF BELIEF NECESSARY TO HUMBLE OURSELVES ENOUGH TO PRAY TO GOD, WE HAVE AN OPEN INVITATION TO ASK FOR HELP WITH OUR DOUBTS.

WE WILL FIGHT TOGETHER;
TOGETHER, WE WILL WIN.
WITH A SON'S LOVE FOR
HIS FATHER,

CHAPTER EIGHT

Press On

November 30, 2017 – Brewster County, Texas

MY HEART HIT a few extra beats per minute as my hands wrung the steering wheel. I looked out the windshield and then at the rearview mirror. It was all the same: dark, indistinguishable desert. *It is 2017. How are you possibly lost in 2017?* I asked myself as we sped down the highway in what I hoped was the right direction.

WHEN I FINISHED my second year as a lawyer, Hannah planned a trip to Big Bend National Park for a weekend of hiking. It was going to be our first visit, and we had booked an adobe house on a dirt road in Terlingua, the legendary ghost town just outside the park. It is a 460-mile drive from San Antonio to Terlingua, 90 percent of which is through wide-open country. We each worked a half-day before leaving, so it was afternoon by the time we headed out.

There are only four turns on the drive. Turn number one is just west of Fort Stockton, 320 miles into the trek. By the time we stopped there for dinner, it was already dark. Hannah was the passenger-seat navigator and guided us through turn number one without a problem. Half an hour later, she guided us through turn number two, just before Alpine. As I made the left at turn number three, we stopped for a passing train.

"The next thing you do is take a right at the fork and we will be there. But it will be a while," she said.

"Got it," I told her. When the train passed and the guard arms lifted, I put the car back into drive and headed south.

I set the cruise control. Between the high beams and the moon, I could see the road stretched out a long way ahead. It whirred beneath the tires. I could see just enough of the land along the side of the road to know it was vast, and the darkness made it seem vaster still. It was like driving across the ocean. There were no points of reference to distinguish the passing miles and minutes. There was nothing except for our car, the road, the moon … and the herd of hogs in the road ahead of me!

I swerved into the oncoming lane and dodged the hogs. The scare snapped me out of my trance. *How long have I been driving?* Hannah had been asleep for a while. I grabbed my phone to check our location: no service. I grabbed Hannah's phone: same. *Did I already go through the fork?* I drove another ten minutes, but there was no fork. So I drove another ten, and then another, but still no fork. You cover a lot of ground in thirty minutes driving eighty miles per hour, and I was growing concerned. *How much further south can it be? We've got to be in Mexico by now.* I looked in the rearview mirror and saw only darkness. I looked at the gas gauge and saw we had half a tank. Then I glanced at Hannah in the passenger seat. *I hope you were right.*

My hands tightened on the wheel as my right foot bounced on the floorboard. *I could turn around*, I thought. We had enough gas to make it back to Alpine. I decided to give it another ten minutes before I woke Hannah to inform her we were lost in the desert. I leaned forward and stared out the windshield. I saw a few dim lights ahead. *Please be Terlingua*, I thought. Then, I saw it: a fork in the road. And next to the fork, a gas station. I veered right and melted back into the driver's seat as a wave of relief washed over me. Hannah woke up as I made the turn.

"We're here," I said with a smile.

We spent a few days exploring the park, including hiking a thirteen-mile loop around the tallest mountain. It was a beautiful and varied trail. Some parts were rocky and wooded, while others were soft dirt and open to the sun. Some parts were well-defined, and others were little more than a worn path in the grass. When we saw cairns—small towers of rocks stacked in descending size—left by other hikers, we felt assured we were on the right path.

By mid-day of the long hike, we were halfway through when we stopped for lunch on a cliff on the backside of the mountain. We let our feet hang off the side as we ate and gazed out over a sea of hills and ravines that faded into the horizon. It was a gorgeous hike. When we rounded the last corner and saw the trail end just fifty feet away, Hannah took off at a sprint. By the time I realized what she was doing, I could not catch her. To this day, she brags about finishing the hike before me.

CHOOSING FAITH IS similar to the trip to Big Bend that weekend. I used to think faith was something outside of my control, like a math problem. I thought my brain took in all the evidence and arguments about God and then spit out a result the way a calculator crunches numbers. If the result was "faith in God not justified," I was no more responsible for that than if my calculator told me four minus two is not one. It was just an involuntary product of an equation.

> TO KNOW SOMETHING IS TO BE CERTAIN IT IS TRUE; TO HAVE FAITH IN SOMETHING IS TO BELIEVE AND TRUST IT IS TRUE.

The problem with that understanding of faith is that it fails to recognize the difference between faith and knowledge. When we are certain something is true, we have knowledge, not faith. To know something is to be *certain* it is true; to have faith in something is to *believe* and *trust* it is true.

Knowledge is good. In fact, so far as it is available to us, knowledge is better than faith because it is a more complete understanding of truth. The problem is we often do not have knowledge.

Take our justice system as an example. As a lawyer, I litigate disputes for a living. When the facts are known, the judge applies the law to the case and resolves the dispute without a trial. Trials occur only when the facts are unknown. In those instances, we do not require the jury to *know* the facts when they issue a verdict. Instead, our legal system instructs the jury to render a verdict based on the preponderance of evidence, which means in favor of whichever side's facts are more likely true, even if only ever so slightly more likely.

It would be ideal to decide each lawsuit with certainty, but when there is an actual dispute between two people in this real world, we do not allow a lack of certainty to indefinitely delay resolution. We decide the case based on belief and trust.

One of the major shifts in my life came when I realized life is not like an academic exercise or logical proof. We exist in motion, and sometimes we are driving a car through the desert in the dark without cell service. When that happens, we do not have the leisure of waiting until we have knowledge to act; we have to choose what we are going to do. On that drive, I could have stopped the car and been certain I was going nowhere or turned around and been certain I was going back where I had come from, but neither of those options would have taken me to Big Bend. If I wanted to make it there, I had to believe and trust I was on the right path.

I am not saying we should ignore knowledge and have faith for the sake of having faith. Several Christians told me things like that when I was an atheist, and it drove me further from God every time I heard it. Faith is not separate from knowledge; it is a choice we make where knowledge ends. Knowledge and faith are like different stretches of the same hiking trail.

Knowledge is the clean-cut part, containing no grass or weeds. When we are hiking that part, we are certain we are on the right path. But as we continue hiking, we see some grass in the path, then some bushes, and then some trees. We come to a point where we cannot be certain we are still on the trail. If we want to move forward, we must choose to hike by faith.

If we continue forward in faith, we will not be certain we are on the trail. But this does not mean we are walking around aimlessly in the wilderness. We are still headed in the general direction the known trail was pointing when it ended, and we may see evidence indicating we are on the right path. We may see some cairns indicating others have walked this trail before. We may even see evidence that someone with far greater knowledge than ours walked through the wilderness with certainty so we could follow in faith. That is exactly what Christianity says we will find.

My life changed when I realized faith is not something that happens to us; it is something we choose. I chose faith in Christianity because I was lost, afraid, hopeless, and desperate for peace. Someone may say a desperate person's judgment is clouded. Perhaps—but a person who has been lost in the wilderness is also best suited to recognize a trail for what it is: something other than the wilderness.

When I came back to Christianity—real Christianity beyond the childhood religion I had walked away from years before—I found it was the best explanation for the big questions that trouble me: *Where did everything come from? Why do I feel like a unique person with free will? Why do I feel there is some law commanding me to use my free will to do good? Why do I often fail to do so? Why do I feel I am always chasing something I cannot find? And why does death seem so unnatural and terrifying?*

In the years since I chose faith, I have learned two hard lessons. First, faith is not a one-time choice. Choosing to take the first step on the trail does not get us to the end. Like hiking, faith is an active exercise. We have to rest, refuel our bodies and minds, and choose to keep moving, even when we do not feel like it. Sometimes, there are no breathtaking views or pleasant breezes, and we have to trudge through the mud and rain.

Second, choosing faith does not give us knowledge. This was an especially difficult lesson for me. I want desperately to be certain about the existence of God, but I still have doubts. Sometimes the doubts are troubling and painful. But then I remind myself a doubt is nothing more than a feeling of uncertainty. And since faith exists only in uncertainty, having doubts is a poor reason for giving up faith.

God's Word about the Source of Faith:

☦ *Jesus said to him, "If you can believe, all things are possible to him who believes." Immediately the father of the child cried out and said with tears, "Lord, I believe; help my unbelief!"*

MARK 9:23–24 NKJV

☦ *Now faith is confidence in what we hope for and assurance about what we do not see.*

HEBREWS 11:1 NIV

☦ *For it is with your heart that you believe and are justified, and it is with your mouth that you profess your faith and are saved. . . .How, then, can they call on the one they have not believed in? And how can they believe in the one of whom they have not heard? And how can they hear without someone preaching to them? . . .Consequently, faith comes from hearing the message, and the message is heard through the word about Christ.*

ROMANS 10:10, 14, 17 NIV

Hey Pops —

You may have already noticed this letter is dated the ninth through the thirteenth. I put the ink on paper on the twelfth and thirteenth, but the content brewed for three days before hand. This letter took longer than others because this one is about my testimony. I suppose you could say I have been writing these words for over three years. But it was not until Friday that I first thought of writing my testimony in one of these letters. And it was not until Sunday, when my pastor preached we should "share what we tasted and why it was good," that I decided for certain to write this.

While devout belief in God was not one of the primary values of our family, you and mom exposed me to God's word enough to enable me to develop some faith. When I moved out on my own, however, I lost that faith. It did not happen all at once, but through years of selfish decisions, I boiled myself down to a staunch atheist. I thought I knew God did not exist. I did not realize how arrogant that was in light of the brilliant thinkers on both sides of the debate. I thought the world contained too much evil to permit the existence of an all-good and all-powerful God. I did not realize

THE SHADOW IN WHICH I SAW THE WORLD WAS CAST BY MY OWN MIND.

As I CONTINUED TO SUCCEED IN SCHOOL AND CAREER WHILE CHOOSING MY ACTIONS BASED ON AN INCREASINGLY SELFISH ETHIC, I BEGAN TO CRACK. THE PRODUCT OF SUCCESS IS NOT A CARE-FREE LIFE, BUT MORE RESPONSIBILITY. I WAS NOT EQUIPPED TO HANDLE IT. I STARTED HAVING PANIC ATTACKS. MY HEART RACED, MY BLOOD RAN ICE COLD, AND THE INSIDE OF MY BODY TRIED TO RIP THROUGH MY SKIN. THE OCCASIONAL PANIC ATTACKS WERE LIKE TEN-FOOT WAVES AND ANXIETY WAS LIKE THE TIDE. IT EBBED AND FLOWED, BUT IT WAS THERE EVERY DAY.

MY PHYSICAL HEALTH FOLLOWED. MY THROAT FELT SWOLLEN TO THE POINT WHERE I PANICKED ABOUT THE ABILITY TO BREATHE. MY HANDS, FEET, AND FACE ALTERNATED BETWEEN TINGLING, BURNING, AND GOING NUMB. MUSCLES ALL OVER MY BODY BEGAN TWITCHING INVOLUNTARILY. MY LEGS BUZZED SO BAD AT NIGHT THAT I WOULD WALK ON MY APARTMENT'S TREADMILL IN THE MIDDLE OF THE NIGHT. MY TESTOSTERONE LEVEL DROPPED LITERALLY OFF THE CHART, MY LYMPH NODES SWELLED SO LARGE A DOCTOR ORDERED ME TO THE EMERGENCY ROOM, AND I BROKE OUT IN SHINGLES. OVER THE COURSE OF A FEW YEARS, I HAD AN

MRI, CAT SCAN, AND DOZENS OF PHYSICAL EXAMS AND BLOOD TESTS. EVERY ONE OF THEM WAS INCONCLUSIVE.

I WAS LIVING TWO LIVES: SUCCESFUL AND FUN-LOVING ON THE OUTSIDE, ANXIOUS AND TERRIFIED ON THE INSIDE. I WAS IN PERPETUAL MOTION; I COULD NOT STOP OR REST BECAUSE MY ANXIETY CONSUMED ME IN STILL AND QUIET PLACES. I THOUGHT I WAS DYING, BUT FORWARD I WENT.

SHORTLY AFTER HANNAH AND I GOT ENGAGED, WE STARTED ATTENDING CHURCH. I HAD NO INTENTION OF BELIEVING IN ANYTHING, BUT I THOUGHT IT WOULD MAKE HANNAH HAPPY AND ME A MORE RESPECTABLE HUSBAND. I ANTICIPATED EMOTION-EVOKING MUSIC AND A SOCIAL-CLUB VIBE. THESE THINGS, I REASONED, WERE WHAT PEOPLE ATTENDED CHURCH FOR; THE ACTUAL MESSAGE WOULD BE EITHER VAGUE PROSPERITY JARGON OR UTTER NONSENSE. I WAS SURPRISED TO FIND THE MESSAGES FOCUSED ON SPECIFIC, CONCRETE PASSAGES FROM THE BIBLE. AND I WAS SHOCKED TO FIND THEY SEEMED NOT AT ALL NONSENSICAL, BUT LOGICAL AND FULL OF THE SORT OF EXPLANATORY VALUE THAT TRUE ACCOUNTS HAVE.

A FEW MONTHS AFTER WE STARTED ATTENDING CHURCH, I WAS HAVING ANOTHER SLEEPLESS NIGHT. MY LEGS WERE BUZZING AND MY MUSCLES WERE TWITCHING. I GOT OUT OF BED AND SPREAD MY YOGA MAT ON THE CONCRETE LIVING ROOM FLOOR.

I tried to stretch the buzz and twitch out of my legs, but there was no improvement. After several minutes of stretching in vain, I gave up and fell face down on my mat. I was physically, mentally, and emotionally exhausted. I was tired of trying and failing to carry the overwhelming burden of my own expectations. I was tired of searching for whatever it was that I longed for and being disappointed each time I realized my latest accomplishment or pleasure was not it. I was tired of the parade of physical ailments and the cold flood of anxiety. I was tired of fear and, most of all, I was tired of being tired. In that moment, face down on my yoga mat in the middle of the night, I was prostrate in every sense of the word. Then, I prayed.

I prayed for the first time in years. I prayed the only four words I could think of: "Thy will be done." I prayed "Thy will be done" over and over again until I found the energy to pray in more detail. I prayed to God that if it was His will for me to die, then His will be done. Everything changed that night. I wept when I felt something I lacked the words to describe. It was not until months later that I read the words for the first time in

PHILIPPIANS 4:6-7 :

Do not worry about anything; instead, pray about everything. Tell God what you need and thank him for all he has done. Then you will experience God's peace, which exceeds all human understanding. His peace will guard your hearts and minds as you live in Christ Jesus.

When I experienced the peace of God that exceeds all understanding, it changed my life. I know you have a physical illness with a specific diagnosis. I am sharing my testimony not because we face the same challenges, but because we have the same answer. God's peace is available to every person in every situation.

We will fight together; together, we will win.

With a son's love for his father,

CHAPTER NINE

Pursue Peace

2011 – Seguin, Texas

A BREEZE STARTED TO rustle the leaves inside my head. *No, no, no,* I thought. I knew what was coming. Ice spread out from my spine around my body as heat radiated from my neck, ears, and face.

My breath shrank, my throat closed, and my heart slammed into my ribs. I tried to talk sensibly to myself, but it was no use. The breeze in my head was now a hurricane, snapping trees in half and ripping roofs from houses. All four of my limbs were tingling.

"GET OUT!" my subconscious shouted at my body. I tried to intervene, but I could not stay. My skin could not contain the storm raging inside me. I was going to explode and die right there in my chair.

I set my pen down on my exam, got up, and tried my best not to run as I left the classroom. I walked into the restroom down the hall and looked at myself in the mirror. I was drenched in sweat.

IT IS HARD to describe a panic attack. I have tried on several occasions in the past ten years. I settled on what you just read, although I still do not think I have fully captured the feeling. Panic attacks are difficult to explain because they are illogical. Panic is the purest, most concentrated form of fear. It occurs when fear has defeated all rationality.

When we panic, the amount of fear we feel is totally disproportionate to whatever is threatening us, but no amount of logical explanation can ameliorate it. For some people, like me, the nightmare grows so dark that the threat—the thing originally feared—becomes irrelevant. Now, you fear the panic. Now, you fear fear itself. When you get to that point, fear owns you.

I have been there. I had my first panic attack when I was nineteen. At first, they were linked to stress. This did not make the panic attacks any less miserable, but it provided some comfort that I could control the panic by doing my best to avoid the stressors.

Then, fear got clever. Fear started to whisper to me that it would be really horrible if I had a panic attack in a situation in which I needed to remain calm. Fear figured out that even if I was not scared of the situation itself, I was scared that having a panic attack in that situation would render me unable to perform.

That is exactly what fear did to me during my philosophy exam in 2011. I was not scared of the exam. I had studied for it. It was a series of essay questions. I read through all the prompts when I received the exam. I knew all the answers. I loved this philosophy class and enjoyed school. My professor was wonderful; we had a great relationship. There was no real doubt in my mind or my professor's that I would get an A. In short, there was nothing to fear—except fear.

As I looked at myself in the bathroom mirror, I was furious and ashamed. Fear owned me. It could take over my life in any situation now. There were no safe places left to hide.

I wiped the sweat off my face and did breathing exercises to calm down. I was able to reduce my anxiety enough to walk back into the classroom and finish the exam, although I felt far from well. I do not remember how long I was in the bathroom, but I was the last person to turn in the exam by a long shot. I apologized to my professor, who showed tremendous compassion and regard for my well-being. Like I said, there was never any threat in that classroom. Fear had ravaged me all on its own.

I CONTINUED STRUGGLING with panic attacks for several years. Fear attacked me on crowded planes and on the highway, on the couch in the afternoon and in bed at night, and in casual settings as well as at work.

When I finally brought my problem to God, I discovered He has an antidote to panic: He calls it peace. The Apostle

Paul called it "God's peace" and said it "exceeds all human understanding" (Philippians 4:7 NIV). Panic and peace are similar in that regard; they both exceed human understanding. Panic and peace are opposite extremes on the same spectrum. Panic is fear in the absence of threat; peace is tranquility in the midst of chaos.

> PANIC IS FEAR IN THE ABSENCE OF THREAT; PEACE IS TRANQUILITY IN THE MIDST OF CHAOS.

God's peace really does exceed my human understanding. I do not know how He changed me from someone who suffered from panic attacks to someone who litigates high-pressure cases for a living, but He did. Before every deposition, trial, hearing, and oral argument, I pray Philippians 4:6–7. I thank God for everything, tell Him what I need, and ask Him for peace. God's peace is the greatest gift I have ever received. You cannot buy it with money, but if you could, I would empty my bank account for it. In my never-ending war against fear, God's peace is my shield and sword. I do not go anywhere without it.

NOTE:

If you are struggling with panic attacks, please do not suffer in silence. Seek help. A pastor can guide you spiritually toward recovery. Doctors and therapists can guide you medically toward recovery. While I do not currently take any medication for anxiety, I did at one point in my life. There is no shame in using medication as one tool in your overall approach to improving mental health. I firmly believe sleep, exercise, and diet have a huge impact on mental health, as I have experienced and as numerous studies have shown. If you are suffering from panic attacks, please know this: you can get better. I encourage you to pray to God, seek professional help, and take an active approach to building a lifestyle conducive to better mental health.

GOD'S WORD TO THE ANXIOUS:

☫ *Don't worry about anything; instead, pray about everything. Tell God what you need, and thank him for all he has done. Then you will experience God's peace, which exceeds anything we can understand. His peace will guard your hearts and minds as you live in Christ Jesus.*

PHILIPPIANS 4:6–7 NLT

☫ *"That is why I tell you not to worry about everyday life— whether you have enough food and drink, or enough clothes to wear. Isn't life more than food, and your body more than clothing? Look at the birds. They don't plant or harvest or store food in barns, for your heavenly Father feeds them. And aren't you far more valuable to him than they are? Can all your worries add a single moment to your life?*

"And why worry about your clothing? Look at the lilies of the field and how they grow. They don't work or make their clothing, yet Solomon in all his glory was not dressed as beautifully as they are. And if God cares so wonderfully for wildflowers that are here today and thrown into the fire tomorrow, he will certainly care for you. Why do you have so little faith?

"So don't worry about these things, saying, 'What will we eat? What will we drink? What will we wear?' These things dominate the thoughts of unbelievers, but your heavenly Father already knows all your needs. Seek the Kingdom of God above all else, and live righteously, and he will give you everything you need.

"So don't worry about tomorrow, for tomorrow will bring its own worries. Today's trouble is enough for today."

MATTHEW 6:25–34 NLT

✝ *Don't be afraid, for I am with you.*
Don't be discouraged, for I am your God.
I will strengthen you and help you.
I will hold you up with my victorious right hand.

ISAIAH 41:10 NLT

Hey Pops —

This is my first letter since Hannah and I returned from Atlanta. Spending time with you and Mom brought me joy. And while I am pleased to resume writing these letters, they are an imperfect substitute for in-person reunion. The Bible, which seems to have words of wisdom for every imaginable situation, speaks to this point. In 2 John 1:12, the Apostle John wrote:

> I have much more to say to you, but I do not want to use paper and ink. Instead, I hope to visit you and talk with you face to face, so that our joy may be complete.

John recognizes joy in communion with others. We sometimes equate happiness with joy, but I think this is a grave error we must avoid.

Happiness is a fragile and volatile feeling determined by external stimuli. We can change from feeling frustrated to happy immediately upon receiving a pay raise, or from stressed to happy as soon as we have a stiff drink. Yet our happiness can leave just as quickly. We can change from feeling happy to angry when a tire blows out, or from happy to depressed if we contract a serious illness. Happiness is not bad; it is good to appreciate happiness when we experience it. But it is dangerous to make happiness our end, because we cannot control the circumstances that determine it. If we live for happiness, there will be droughts that leave us devastated in thirst.

Joy is different. Joy is a durable and stable state of being controlled by our will. Unlike happiness, joy neither comes nor goes with haste. We build joy by recognizing our faith gives us hope, and then marching toward that hope by loving God and others. Misfortune and illness cannot tear down our joy because our joy is not conditioned on good fortune or health.

Jesus taught the difference between happiness and joy at the well in Samaria. In John 4:13-14, Jesus told the woman at the well:

> Everyone who drinks this water will be thirsty again, but whoever drinks the water I give them will never thirst. Indeed, the water I give them will become in them a spring of water welling up to eternal life.

When we live for happiness, we have to go to

THE WELL EVERYDAY IN THIRST AND HOPE THERE IS WATER. BUT WHEN WE LIVE FOR JOY IN CHRIST, WE DO NOT THIRST EVEN WHEN THE WELL IS DRY.

WE WILL FIGHT TOGETHER; TOGETHER, WE WILL WIN. WITH A SON'S LOVE FOR HIS FATHER,

CHAPTER TEN

Seek Joy

2016 – San Antonio, Texas

I PULLED THE BAKING pan from the oven and set it on the stovetop. I looked down at the sandy batter as I combed through it with a fork. *This can't be right*, I thought to myself. I tasted a pinch. *Definitely not right.*

***

DURING MY SECOND winter in law school, I learned about ice fog. I was cramming for finals when the weather got so cold and wet the entire city froze. There was ice everywhere—on the trees, the sides of buildings, and the roads, including the steep exit out of my apartment complex. I watched one of my neighbors slide backward down the ramp of the parking lot as he tried to drive out. I was not going anywhere. I hunkered down inside, put on a pot of coffee, and got down to the exciting task of studying for my business enterprises exam.

What I really need with my cup of coffee on this cold day of studying is a cookie, I thought as I got up from the desk before I had even started. I opened the pantry and looked around. I knew there were no cookies, but I looked anyway, just to be sure. If I wanted cookies with my coffee, I was going to have to bake them myself.

I had never baked cookies from scratch before, but since I was supposed to be studying for a final, what better time to try something new? I spent a few minutes researching recipes, but each one I found called for ingredients I did not have—like flour and sugar.

After reading through five recipes, I felt like I had a good grasp on the general outline of cookie baking. I grabbed some raw oatmeal and threw it in a bowl with some other ingredients, stirred the mix, pinched out globs of batter, and pushed them down into circles on a pan. When the pan was full from edge to edge, I slid it into the oven and wiped my hands in satisfaction. Twelve minutes later, I pulled a tray of golden-brown cookies from the oven.

I let the cookies cool for a few minutes as I poured a fresh cup of coffee and got ready to revel in my culinary genius. I set a plate of cookies on the desk next to my textbook and highlighters. I took a seat in my chair, grabbed a cookie, and bit in. I drew my hand away from my mouth and glared at the cookie. It was terrible. I did not know something that looked so good could taste so awful. It was bland and bitter at the same time and coated my mouth with a mystery film that lingered for hours.

It was a few years before I was ready to bake again. I was living in San Antonio and decided to bake a cake while Hannah was out one day. I had learned my lesson about baking without a recipe, so this time, I found a recipe and made sure I had all the ingredients I needed. I had the eggs, sugar, milk, butter, and flour—and not just any flour. I had coconut flour, which I was sure would give my cake a hint of delicious coconut flavor.

I followed the recipe with exacting precision. I measured everything with actual measuring cups and spoons, added the ingredients in the correct order, and whisked for the specified time. Everything was great until I read the next instruction: "Pour the batter into the pan." I looked down at my batter, then back at the picture on the screen. There was also a video included in the recipe, which showed a river of batter flowing from a bowl into the baking pan. I reached down into the bowl of clumpy sand in front of me and stirred it with my fingers. I pulled them out, bone dry. *It probably just needs to cook some*, I thought as I dumped the batter into the pan. I pushed down on the batter and slapped it to pack it into place.

I slid the pan into the oven and waited. Half an hour later, I pulled it out. There was no discernible difference between what I had put into the oven and what I had taken out. I slid the pan back in and set the timer for another half an hour. The same thing came out of the oven again.

One more time, I thought as I slid the pan back into the oven. When I pulled it out thirty minutes later, nothing had changed. I grabbed a fork and raked through what looked like the Sahara Desert in a baking pan. I pinched a little of the sand between my thumb and fingers and dropped it into my mouth for a taste test.

I coughed as it sucked the moisture from my salivary glands and left my tongue stuck to the roof of my mouth. It was the driest thing I had ever eaten. Helicopters could drop it over flooded cities to dry the streets. I turned the oven off.

I WILL NEVER win a baking contest, but there are a few things about baking I now know as well as anyone in the world, such as the absorbent properties of coconut flour. There are some topics in life about which we leave a lot of wisdom unsaid because we feel unqualified to speak. C.S. Lewis wrote, "[I]t is fools, they say, who learn by experience. But since they do at least learn, let a fool bring his experience into the common stock that wiser men profit by it." [1]

When it comes to both baking and faith, I am a fool who has learned from experience. In the past, I tried to build a life with a lot of bad ingredients—things that never make good batter no matter how you mix them, like lying and then drinking to numb the guilt. I was in pain but not too surprised when I ended up a wreck.

What surprised me was what happened when I tried to build a life with good ingredients, like academic success, a promising career, a nice apartment downtown, good friends, and the love of a wonderful woman. What did I get when I mixed those? Hot sand.

---

[1]   C.S. Lewis, afterword to *The Pilgrim's Regress*, 1933; reprinted (New York: Eerdmans, 1992).

Without God in the mix, all the good ingredients were wasted on me. I have rarely been so scared as when I looked around, realized I had everything I wanted, and still felt empty. When I built my life around obtaining happiness, I opened the door for fear. It whispered to me: "You got what you wanted, and you are not happy. You will never be happy."

But I was just one ingredient away from something better. When I chose faith and made God the main ingredient in my life, everything changed. I had rejected God and worshiped myself until I was in a place so dark I thought hope was a cruel joke.

But it was not. God rescued me from the darkness, opened my eyes to see the truth, and opened my heart to love Him and others. My fool's wisdom about faith comes not only from self-inflicted painful experiences, but from the incomparably triumphant experience of escaping the darkness.

I experienced joy, and when I built my life around it, I closed the door on fear. Since then, I have discovered something about the relationship between joy and happiness. Joy produces happiness, not the other way around.

> JOY PRODUCES HAPPINESS, NOT THE OTHER WAY AROUND.

Getting pay raises and moving into a more luxurious home has made me happy but never led me to joy. I can feel just as empty in a mansion as in a shack. But experiencing and choosing joy has made me more likely to feel happy about the things that happen in my life. With God in the mix, all the other ingredients in my life came together and tasted better than ever before.

God's Word about Happiness and Joy:

✝ *Jesus answered, "Everyone who drinks this water will be thirsty again, but whoever drinks the water I give them will never thirst. Indeed, the water I give them will become in them a spring of water welling up to eternal life."*

JOHN 4:13–14 NIV

✝ *I denied myself nothing my eyes desired;*
I refused my heart no pleasure.
My heart took delight in all my labor,
and this was the reward for all my toil.
Yet when I surveyed all that my hands had done
and what I had toiled to achieve,
everything was meaningless, a chasing after the wind;
nothing was gained under the sun.

ECCLESIASTES 2:10–11 NIV

✝ *Though you have not seen him, you love him; and even though you do not see him now, you believe in him and are filled with an inexpressible and glorious joy, for you are receiving the end result of your faith, the salvation of your souls.*

1 PETER 1:8–9 NIV

Hey Pops —

I have never told you how grateful I am that you taught me to love sport. You had little to say about literature, art, or music. But sport, you taught me, is the great drama of the human pursuit of excellence. Sport requires the discipline of focused training in preparation, and encourages ~~the~~ execution beyond perceived limits in performance. This transcendance into the impossible is the virtue of sport; it is the truth in the theme of a classic work of literature; it is the ineffable message in the beauty of a piano or painted canvas.

This is why we love sports and use sport analogies to convey ideas. In Hebrews 12:1-4, the Bible says:

> Therefore, since we are surrounded by such a huge crowd of witnesses to the life of faith, let us strip off every weight that slows us down, especially the sin that so easily trips us up. And let us run with endurance the race God has set before us. We do this by keeping our eyes on Jesus, the champion who initiates and perfects

OUR FAITH. BECAUSE OF THE JOY AWAITING HIM, HE ENDURED THE CROSS, DISREGARDING ITS SHAME. NOW HE IS SEATED IN THE PLACE OF HONOR BESIDE GOD'S THRONE. THINK OF ALL THE HOSTILITY HE ENDURED FROM SINFUL PEOPLE; THEN YOU WILL NOT BECOME WEARY AND GIVE UP. AFTER ALL, YOU HAVE NOT YET GIVEN YOUR LIVES IN THE STRUGGLE AGAINST SIN.

EACH OF OUR LIVES IS LIKE A RACE, AND RACES ARE MEANT TO BE RUN. JUST AS ATHLETES INSPIRE OTHERS THROUGH THEIR FEATS, WE CAN INSPIRE THE WITNESSES TO OUR LIVES THROUGH OUR FAITH. JUST AS ATHLETES DO NOT STOP WITH TIME ON THE CLOCK OR MILES LEFT AHEAD OF THEM, WE MUST COMPLETE OUR RACES WITH ENDURANCE. WHEN WE FEEL BURDENED, WE PRAY TO GOD FOR HELP TO STRIP OFF THE WEIGHTS SLOWING US DOWN. WHEN WE FEEL WEARY, WE PRAY TO GOD FOR THE STRENGTH OF JESUS CHRIST WHO RAN HIS RACE TO THE END.

WE WILL FIGHT TOGETHER;
TOGETHER, WE WILL WIN.
WITH A SON'S LOVE FOR
HIS FATHER,

CHAPTER ELEVEN

Endure Together

May 16, 2020 – San Antonio, Texas

I LOOKED AT THE lime green bottles strapped to my hands. One was empty and the other was close to it. I looked at my GPS watch. We had covered thirty-nine miles and were on our second-to-last leg of the fifty-mile run. Cloud cover had protected us through the morning and early afternoon, but it was gone, and the sun had free reign over the sky. We would restock water at my house before the last leg, but that was still two miles away; the single swallow of water remaining in my bottle would not be enough to get me home. There was a gas station on the next block, but I did not have my wallet. I was not even wearing a shirt. I was clothed in shoes, shorts, sweat, and stench. I looked over at Davey J.

"Do you have your debit card on you?" I asked.

"Yes," he answered in a raspy voice.

"The gas station. Buy us a water. A big one," I panted.

I stood in a sliver of shade next to the gas station and stretched my calves as I waited for him.

I GOT INTO endurance athletics when I decided to run fifty miles on my thirtieth birthday. I ran track in high school but was a sprinter. I cannot recall ever running more than one mile until I ran a 5K in my mid-twenties, and that seemed like a long race. No one knew me as an endurance athlete—because I was not one—and when I told people about my plan to run fifty miles, the most common response was: "Why?"

My answer was simple. I wanted to endure something I thought was impossible. When my father got sick, he received a treatment regimen that seemed impossible to endure: radiation every morning, Monday through Friday, and chemotherapy every Friday for eight weeks. And the reward for persevering through those brutal weeks? A highly invasive surgery to remove a section of his esophagus. Make it through all of that, pray to be in remission, and start trying to learn how to eat again.

I did not want to be on the sideline. I wanted to endure my own impossible challenge with him. There was nothing in this world I could subject myself to that would rival his challenge, but running fifty miles seemed like a reasonable substitute.

There was a trail run in a new Texas state park scheduled for the exact day of my thirtieth birthday. I started training as my father endured his treatment. On several weekends, I flew to Atlanta on Thursday, sat next to him during his treatment on Friday, then ran ten miles on Saturday morning in the neighborhood near my parents' apartment.

Four months before the race, I was stuck just over the ten-mile mark. I could push to thirteen or fourteen miles, but then I would crash—hard. I would be too sick to eat for hours.

Hannah suggested I work with a coach, and that is when I met Coach Brandi. She was a hardcore triathlete who had trained for and completed a triathlon while fighting and beating cancer. She was a perfect fit. She put me on a heart rate-based training plan and taught me about the science of training for an endurance race. It turns out my prior approach of running as hard as I could until I felt violently ill was not the ideal method.

I had to walk a lot during the first few weeks of my new training plan to stay in the proper heart rate zones, and it was frustrating. I did not feel like I was making any progress. But with Coach Brandi's guidance, I built up endurance through repetition. I eventually got to the point where my heart was stronger than my legs, and I wished I was back to needing walk breaks for my heart rate.

In the weeks leading up to the race, I set a new personal record-long run each weekend: fifteen miles, eighteen miles, twenty miles, twenty-three miles, and finally, twenty-five miles. Between these longer weekend efforts, I mixed in shorter, weekday morning runs. I had left my comfort zone behind many months ago, and by this point, my feet hurt from my first step on the tile floor next to my bed each morning to my last step in the evening, every day.

When the trail race I had been training for was canceled due to COVID-19, there was no way I was wasting all the work I had put in. I mapped out a course in San Antonio on my training loops. Davey J had signed up to run the trail race with me. I asked him if he still wanted to run on the makeshift San Antonio course. I already knew the answer. Davey J is nuts; he would run barefoot over broken glass with me.

DAVEY J WALKED out from the gas station with a two-liter bottle of water in his hand. He walked over and joined me in the sliver of shade. He took a drag and passed it to me. We drank about half of it on the spot and poured the rest into our hand-held bottles. Then, we stepped back out into the sun.

You have a lot of time to think during a fifty-mile run. The day before the race, Coach Brandi had told me: "Remember your why." When you are exhausted and in severe pain, you need to know why you are going forward. If you do not know your why, you will not be able to think of any good reason to keep going. All you will be able to think about is the pain in your joints and the chafing on your skin in places no one should have chafing. I knew my why. I wanted to endure what I thought was impossible.

Davey J and I had started walking the uphill stretches a few miles back. Now we were walking half of the flat stretches as well. We had a mile and a half to make it back to my house for our final break, and I was at a wall.

You hit several walls in a long race. They are points when the amount of energy remaining in your body seems insufficient to get through the remaining miles. People do not quit races when they are having a runner's high and the breeze is brushing their skin. People quit races when they feel like they have two miles left in their legs, but there are twelve miles left to run. But a wall is not the end of the road; it is just a wall. And if you tear the wall down, there is open road on the other side.

There is a prayer I say hours into a race when I am at a wall. It is a combination of various scriptural verses, and the exact wording varies each time I say it, but it goes something like this: "God, thank You for everything You have blessed me with. I cannot complete this race on my own. Please help me draw on the power of the Holy Spirit who lives within me, the same power that raised Jesus from the grave. When I live by Spirit and not flesh alone, I will run and not grow weary, I will walk and not be faint. I can do all things through Christ who strengthens me."

I prayed. Then, one of my friends drove by in his car and shouted words of encouragement. Davey J and I were pushing forward. I broke through the wall.

We turned onto my street and ran the last block back to the house. Twenty people stood outside on the lawn and cheered us in for our final break. Hannah had secretly assembled a support squad of friends and family, some of whom had driven hours to be there. I was exhausted, and the outpouring of love overwhelmed me.

Davey J and I had eight miles left. It was mid-afternoon, hot, and humid, but our last loop was flat and partly shaded. Hannah wheeled her bike out of the house. She was riding with us the last eight miles. I laced my shoes up, loaded my running belt with supplies, and asked my brother to spray a fresh coat of sunscreen on me. Then Davey J and I headed out as everyone cheered for us.

I thought I had felt all possible leg pains during my training. I was wrong. Every left step of the final eight miles sent searing pain down the top of my foot. The tight and swollen strands in my right Achilles vibrated as they rubbed against each other. Both of my hip flexors were numb and powerless. I was spread thinner than I had ever been before, like a wet tissue in the sun. But walking hurt just as much as running, so I ran as much as my legs would allow. I thought of how my father battled through chemo and radiation. I thought of all he endured in his metaphorical race. Surely, I could endure eight more miles in this literal race.

We ran through downtown, then wound through the beautiful, tree-shaded streets of South Town. Hannah rode ahead on her bike to check intersections.

"These guys are on mile forty-four of fifty!" she yelled to people walking by. Some of them cheered; some of them just looked shocked. The look on their faces confirmed my why. I was proving to myself and others we can endure the impossible.

Every time my watch dinged for another mile completed, I called it out, just above a whisper, and Hannah echoed the number in a shout followed by an enthusiastic "Woo!" When we passed in front of the Alamo on the way back north, we were at mile forty-seven. Coach Brandi was parked on the side of the road ahead of us. She gave Davey J and me each a bottle of water to drink and then poured two more over our heads. By the time we hit mile forty-nine, we were a pack of five.

Davey J was a half-step behind me, clipping my heels; Hannah was on the bike going ahead and looping back around, and Coach Brandi and Sarah were running alongside us.

We turned onto my street. There were three blocks left. I had never even run a standard 26.2-mile marathon before today. Each of the forty thousand steps over the last five hours had been a new personal record. And now there were just three blocks left.

Hannah rode ahead. Coach Brandi and Sarah dropped off to the left. Davey J pulled up alongside me. He could have finished earlier, but he did not. He had run step for step with me for over ten hours. My watch dinged, and we both heard it. Fifty miles. We looked at each other. We did not need to say anything. We looked forward. My brother and brother-in-law were holding a makeshift, toilet-paper finish line stretched across the street. Behind that was a semicircle of family and friends clapping, cheering, holding signs, blowing air horns, and ringing cow bells. We covered the final steps the same way we had been running since 6:05 a.m., stride for stride. I threw my arms up overhead as Davey J and I crossed the finish line.

THAT NIGHT, AS I sat on the front porch where so many family members and friends had spent their day supporting me, I thought little about my run. I anticipated reliving every step in my mind. Instead, I could not stop thinking about everyone who had come to encourage me, and I wondered, *Why do we gather for races?*

To play baseball, you need at least a few other people to pitch and field, but not to run; you can do that alone. You might say we have races to see who has the most speed and best endurance. This may be true for high school track meets and the Olympics, but not the majority of races. Take running a marathon, for example. Many marathons have more than fifteen thousand participants each year, and the largest have nearly fifty thousand. The average person running a marathon is not competing to be first, fifth, or 500th. The average person runs a marathon to complete, not to compete.

But if it is not for competition, why do tens of thousands gather together to run in dense crowds when each of them could run on their own in open space? Why did my family and friends spend a Saturday standing in my yard, cheering me in and out of breaks every nine miles?

I think we gather for races because life is like a race; each person has to run his own, but we run them together. We cannot take on each other's burdens or appropriate each other's triumphs. If you have cancer, no one else can bear the disease for you. We can help you—encourage you, bring you dinner, and cut your grass while you are in the hospital—but we cannot take on your burden.

If you face your medical battle with tremendous courage, we cannot appropriate your triumph. You can thank us—for the encouragement, meals, and a manicured lawn—but you cannot confer to us the triumph of your courage.

We cannot run each other's races, but we can run with each other. We can cheer for each other. We can help each

> WE CANNOT RUN
> EACH OTHER'S
> RACES, BUT WE
> CAN RUN WITH
> EACH OTHER.

other tear down our walls and do things we thought were impossible. We can help each other overcome fear. And I think that is exactly what God wants: for us to be the answers to each other's prayers. We pray for courage to face our cancer battles, and we get letters from our sons; we pray for strength to finish our races, and we get encouragement from our friends.

GOD'S WORD ABOUT ENDURANCE:

✟ *Therefore, since we are surrounded by such a huge crowd of witnesses to the life of faith, let us strip off every weight that slows us down, especially the sin that so easily trips us up. And let us run with endurance the race God has set before us. We do this by keeping our eyes on Jesus, the champion who initiates and perfects our faith. Because of the joy awaiting him, he endured the cross, disregarding its shame. Now he is seated in the place of honor beside God's throne. Think of all the hostility he endured from sinful people; then you won't become weary and give up. After all, you have not yet given your lives in the struggle against sin.*

HEBREWS 12:1–4 NLT

✟ *May the God who gives endurance and encouragement give you the same attitude of mind toward each other that Christ Jesus had, so that with one mind and one voice you may glorify the God and Father of our Lord Jesus Christ.*

ROMANS 15:5–6 NIV

✟ *Then Moses summoned Joshua and said to him in the presence of all Israel, "Be strong and courageous, for you must go with this people into the land that the LORD swore to their ancestors to give them, and you must divide it among them as their inheritance. The LORD himself goes before you and will be with you; he will never leave you nor forsake you. Do not be afraid; do not be discouraged."*

DEUTERONOMY 31:7–8 NIV

Hey Pops —

It is hard to believe you are already half-way through you first phase of treatment. I remember grandparents telling me that time speeds up as you age. Those words seemed so foreign as I spent summers that felt like lifetimes and waited ages for my driver's license. As I approach thirty years of age next year, I am starting to understand.

When life seems like it is moving faster than I can track or changing more than I can adjust, I am grateful God gave us a four-sentence summary of the Bible. In Matthew 22:37-40, Jesus responded to the Pharisees' question of which commandments are the most important:

Jesus replied, "'You must love the Lord your God with all your heart, all your soul, and all your mind.' This is the first and greatest commandment. A second is equally important: 'Love your neighbor as yourself.' The entire law and all the demands of the prophets are based on these two commandments."

That summary, love God and love your neighbor, should serve as our guiding principle as the page on the calendar, address on our

LICENSES, AND CHALLENGES BEFORE US CHANGE. IT IS A CONSTANT COMMANDMENT AND A CONSTANT SOURCE OF FULFILLMENT. WE ARE NOT FOCUSED HERE ON LOVE THE EMOTION, BUT LOVE THE ACTION. AS C.S. LEWIS SAID, "LOVE IS NOT AN AFFECTIONATE FEELING, BUT A STEADY WISH FOR THE LOVED PERSON'S ULTIMATE GOOD, AS LONG AS IT CAN BE OBTAINED." WE CANNOT CONTROL OUR EMOTIONS, BUT THAT DOES NOT MEAN WE HAVE TO ALLOW OUR EMOTIONS TO CONTROL US. WE CAN CHOOSE LOVE AND WE SHOULD, EVERYDAY.

WE WILL FIGHT TOGETHER; TOGETHER, WE WILL WIN. WITH A SON'S LOVE FOR HIS FATHER,

Share Love

November 13, 2015 – Cabo San Lucas, Mexico

THE WAITRESS SET the flower-covered plate on the table, and my heart burst into a sprint. I got out of my chair and felt the cool sand compress under my knee. I slid my right hand into my pocket and dug for the ring. I watched my girlfriend pull the note from the flowers and start reading, her glossy eyes shimmering in the mix of white moonlight and orange, tiki-torch glow. My pulse thumped in my ears like a bass drum while the waves hissed like a snare. The fate of my life was on the line for the second time in a week. *Please say yes,* I thought as I waited.

NOVEMBER 2015 WAS a milestone in my life, the end of three long months at the end of three long years.

The Texas Bar Exam is sandwiched between two three-month periods. The first is the infamous study period. It starts in May at the end of your last semester of law school and stretches to the moment you walk into the test center in late July. There is an entire industry devoted to providing resources to examinees during these three months. There are prep courses, review books, practice tests, sample essays, and guides with suggested living arrangements and daily schedules for the summer. If you want more help, you can hire a private tutor. If you need money to pay the private tutor, you can take out one of the loans lenders market to examinees. If you have a need, there is a company with a product or service.

The second period is less well known: It is the waiting period. It starts when you walk out of the testing center on the last day and stretches until the first week of November when the state releases the exam results. Unlike the study period, there are few if any resources to help examinees in the waiting period. Some examinees take extended vacations and refuse to think about it anymore. Others argue in online forums about the nuances of answers to essay questions. After three years of squeezing two-hour reading assignments into thirty-minute windows, followed by three months of cramming for the exam, law graduates suddenly have too much of the world's most limited resource: time.

I did well during the study period. I was nervous about taking the exam, like everyone else, but I followed a strict routine to keep myself focused and moving. Each day, I studied all morning on my laptop, worked out while thinking about the materials, cooked a lunch fit for a king, and studied in the afternoon at the apartment pool. I was done by 6:00 p.m., in time to spend the evening with my girlfriend. That was my life for twelve weeks.

On the last week in July, I reported to the testing center for three days. Taking the exam was stressful—and hot when the AC went out on the second day—but I felt prepared and was excited to knock it out. When I left the testing center on the third day, I was sure I had passed.

Then, I entered the waiting period. Just one week after the exam, I went back to my job as a law clerk because I needed the money. After a few weeks back on the job, I was still feeling confident, although I was second-guessing one or two of my essay answers.

By September, my second-guessing had evolved into skepticism, and by October, I was sure I had failed. I started losing sleep, reading the online exam-related forums (which were a dark place by that point), and researching how to register for the next exam in February. I limped into November like a prisoner awaiting his sentence.

I had spent three grueling years in law school and studied for thousands and thousands of hours. I owed somewhere between a nice car and a shabby house in student loans. On top of that, I had just purchased, on credit, an engagement ring worth several times more than my next most valuable possession—my old, white, stick-shift pickup with manual locks, manual windows, and a dented, forest-green tailgate. I would have waited to buy the ring until after the exam results came out, but I wanted to be sure I had it in time for the weekend getaway to Mexico I had planned with my girlfriend for the following weekend, which I also bought on credit. I had a lot riding on the exam results.

TO MY TREMENDOUS relief, I passed. I reveled in my accomplishment for a few days before I started to feel uneasy again. The pending exam results had occupied so much of my attention I had not realized how nervous I was about proposing. I had not told a soul about my plan, had solicited no feedback or second opinions, and considered the odds for my girlfriend's response to be about 60 percent yes, 40 percent no, which is better than 50/50, but less than ideal for a proposal. Two days before we flew to Mexico, I met her father for a beer, told him of my intentions, and asked for his blessing.

"What if she says no?" he asked.

It would have been a funny joke, had the odds been better. For the second time in eight days, I would be waiting to hear life-defining results. I decided I needed to give my odds a last-minute boost, so I emailed the resort in Mexico, explained my plan to propose at dinner, and asked for a good table. The concierge told me I could have a table on the beach for $35. I thought that was a little pricey just to be a few feet closer to the water, but I was not in a position to say no. To this day, it is the best $35 I have ever spent.

My girlfriend and I arrived at the airport the morning of the big day, which was, of course, Friday the thirteenth. I felt like an international diamond smuggler as I walked through security, terrified the TSA agent would grab my backpack, pull the ring out, and ask me what it was. There were a lot of places I could have proposed, but the security line in the airport was not high on my list.

We made it through security and to Mexico without a hitch. When we arrived at the resort, I snuck down to the restaurant to confer with the waitstaff one last time. I knew I was going to be too nervous and emotional to speak, so I had written my proposal. I gave the note to the waitstaff and asked them to deliver it between the first and second course.

A few hours later, my girlfriend and I went down to the restaurant for dinner. We walked past the host stand where I had dropped off the note, through the restaurant, and down a set of wooden stairs. I felt her hand tighten on my arm. The steps before us were lined with candles and ended in the sand, which had been swept smooth as a stiffly starched shirt for hundreds of feet in each direction. There, in the center of the beach, beneath the moonlight, bathed in the sound of foamy waves, was one table for two. We had hundreds of feet of prime Mexican beach all to ourselves. (I told you it was the best $35 I ever spent!)

I do not remember the food or wine from that evening, but I remember when the waitress delivered the note on a plate covered in flower petals. I remember the feeling of the sand on my knee as I reached into my pocket for the ring. And I remember when Hannah whispered, "Yes," with teary eyes and a trembling, outstretched left hand. We spent the next two days with our phones turned off, enjoying our engagement, just the two of us on a beach in Mexico, before anyone else knew.

BUYING A WEEKEND getaway to Mexico and an engagement ring on credit before I knew the results of the exam was objectively not a wise financial decision. I could not afford the trip or the ring, was not sure I would pass the exam, and was not even sure Hannah would say yes. Two "no" answers that week would have left me in a rough spot.

But I am glad I did it the way I did because it taught me something: Love is fear's greatest weakness. Years later, I learned the Bible states this truth in no uncertain terms: "There is no fear in love. But perfect love drives out fear." (1 John 4:18 NIV).

I do not claim to have "perfect love" for others, nor to be free of fear. But I have found love and fear to be inversely related. The more I am focused on loving someone else, the less fear I feel. The less I am focused on the man in the mirror, the more courage I have.

The Bible says each of us has received perfect love from God. We have the opportunity and duty to accept it and share it with others. We may not do it perfectly, but I believe we shine God's love most brightly in places fear has darkened. That is why love is fear's greatest weakness—the darker fear makes a scene, the brighter love can shine.

> LOVE IS FEAR'S GREATEST WEAKNESS—THE DARKER FEAR MAKES A SCENE, THE BRIGHTER LOVE CAN SHINE.

The beautiful thing about love is that it drives fear out of both the person giving and the person receiving it. Love encourages the scared to perform feats of heroism. We hear this from soldiers who explain that their courage to enter the line of fire comes from their love of the men and women standing next to them rather than an abstract concept or self-glory.

Love also provides for those in need by inspiring others to help. We see this in the good Samaritan who helps a stranded motorist change a tire and the teenager who invites a new student to sit with her at lunch.

More often than not, shared love will drive fear from both the giver and the recipient. We need other people *we can help* just as much as we need other people *to help us*. I have seen this day after day in the nine years since Hannah said "yes" on the beach in Mexico, and I saw it in the words I wrote in every letter to my father.

GOD'S WORD ABOUT LOVE:

✝ *"Do not hate a fellow Israelite in your heart. Rebuke your neighbor frankly so you will not share in their guilt.*

"Do not seek revenge or bear a grudge against anyone among your people, but love your neighbor as yourself. I am the Lord."

LEVITICUS 19:17–18 NIV

✝ *Jesus replied, "'You must love the Lord your God with all your heart, all your soul, and all your mind.' This is the first and greatest commandment. A second is equally important: 'Love your neighbor as yourself.' The entire law and all the demands of the prophets are based on these two commandments."*

MATTHEW 22:37–40 NLT

✝ *There is no fear in love. But perfect love drives out fear, because fear has to do with punishment. The one who fears is not made perfect in love.*

We love because he first loved us. Whoever claims to love God yet hates a brother or sister is a liar. For whoever does not love their brother and sister, whom they have seen, cannot love God, whom they have not seen. And he has given us this command: Anyone who loves God must also love their brother and sister.

1 JOHN 4:18–21 NIV

Hey Pops —

As I write this, I am 35,000 feet above ground, moving at 530 miles per hour, headed to see you for the weekend. Flying is one of those things that amazes me, when I think about it. When you fly a dozen or more times per year, you lose perspective of the sheer marvel of engineering you are taking part in. I think life is like this. The common seems like mere background because it is common. We focus on holidays, foreign destinations, and our next milestone of achievement. We treat the other 95% of the calendar, our home city, and our daily work as the filler between the important things.

But if we stop to think about what we are doing at any given moment, I think we will find the common in our life is remarkable. Right now, for example, I am making a series of small marks on a page to transfer thoughts from my mind to yours. I do not have to make a sound and you do not have to see me; we can communicate with nothing more than a few sheets of paper with ink marks on them.

When we look around this world and study ourselves, we find the most remarkable thing inside of us: our free will. The existence of our free will is a miracle. Everything

ELSE IN THE WORLD IS DETERMINED BY THE NATURAL EVENTS PRECEDING IT. YET WE HAVE FREE WILL WHILE SIMULTANEOUSLY BEING A PART OF THE NATURAL WORLD. I BELIEVE FREE WILL IS THE CHARACTERISTIC GOD WAS REFERRING TO IN GENESIS 1:26, WHEN GOD SAID, "LET US MAKE MANKIND IN OUR IMAGE, IN OUR LIKENESS." THE APOSTLE JOHN REMARKED AT THE INCREDIBLE GIFT OF OUR FREE WILL, IN 1 JOHN 3:1:

> SEE WHAT LOVE THE FATHER HAS LAVISHED ON US, THAT WE SHOULD BE CALLED CHILDREN OF GOD! AND THAT IS WHAT WE ARE!

YET, JOHN GOES ON TO SAY, EVEN OUR FREE WILL AS CHILDREN OF GOD DOES NOT COMPARE TO OUR FUTURE:

> NOW WE ARE CHILDREN OF GOD, AND WHAT WE WILL BE HAS NOT YET BEEN MADE KNOWN. BUT WE KNOW THAT WHEN CHRIST APPEARS, WE SHALL BE LIKE HIM, FOR WE SHALL SEE HIM AS HE IS.

WHEN OUR LIVES SEEM BLEAK, WE SHOULD REMEMBER THE WORLD IS FULL OF BEAUTIFUL AND AMAZING CREATIONS, INCLUDING US. WE HAVE THE OPPORTUNITY TO CHOOSE, BY FREE WILL, TO LOVE GOD, LOVE OTHERS, AFFIRM THE GOODNESS OF GOD'S CREATION, AND PROCLAIM WITH HOPE

OUR SALVATION THROUGH JESUS CHRIST.
WE CAN AND SHOULD DO THIS EVERYDAY
AND EVERYWHERE, IN THE OFFICE ON A
TUESDAY AFTERNOON, ON A BEACH DURING A
WEEK-LONG VACATION, EVEN IN THE HOSPITAL
RECEIVING CANCER TREATMENTS.

WE WILL FIGHT TOGETHER;
TOGETHER, WE WILL WIN.
WITH A SON'S LOVE FOR
HIS FATHER,

Ride Wind

October 10, 2015 – Albuquerque, New Mexico

THE PILOT FEATHERED the flame thrower as we continued our descent. I had watched him operate the hot air balloon with absolute certainty over the last hour, as we drifted for miles. But something was different now. His face was tense, and his eyes were scanning the ground all around us.

We had been one of the first balloons to take off and were among the first balloons to descend. I looked back at the sky full of balloons behind us. One of them, a few hundred feet away, descended too quickly, and the wicker basket containing the passengers and pilot snagged a power line. After several tense seconds, the basket slipped free, but there was no way for the huge oval balloon to avoid hitting the line. It partially wrapped around it, then slid off. Stunned, I watched the misshapen and deflated balloon sink rapidly behind the trees on the horizon. From our position, it was hard to judge how far it had fallen, but I knew it was a lot further than I wanted to fall.

I had felt uneasy ever since the safety briefing that morning, but it was not until this moment, in mid-air, that I realized just how dangerous hot air balloon landings are.

I looked back at our pilot. He was no longer scanning the ground around us. His eyes were locked onto the street and field we were fast approaching.

"My ground crew is not here," he said. "Everyone hold on!"

I put Hannah in between my arms, grabbed the rail of the basket with both hands, and braced for impact.

"THIS IS THE final call for passengers Kyle Zunker and Hannah Reeves. Your flight has boarded. The gate will close in two minutes," the voice announced over the airport intercom.

I looked back at Hannah. She was still waiting for the security conveyor belt to spit out her backpack. She waved me on, and I was off. I dashed between the sleepy travelers stumbling through the terminal. *It's too early for this*, I thought as my bag bounced against my back. I saw the gate—the one with no passengers waiting in the chairs—and bounded up to the desk.

"I'm Kyle Zunker," I said and caught my breath. "My girlfriend is Hannah Reeves. She's right behind me." The lady in the uniform did not flinch.

"I'll give her one more minute," she said.

I turned, walked back a few steps, and peered down the terminal. Five seconds passed, then ten, then fifteen. This was not a great start to our weekend getaway. We had reservations for a sunrise ride at the Albuquerque International Balloon Fiesta early the next morning. Riding in a hot air balloon was on Hannah's bucket list, and I did not know if we would make it to Albuquerque in time if we missed our flight.

I scanned the faces of everyone shuffling down the hallway. Then, I saw her, one hand on each backpack strap, gliding down the terminal. We scanned our boarding passes, high-fived each other, and hurried down the empty skybridge. We turned the sharp right onto the plane and saw a sea of red-eyed, weary faces. They glanced up from phones and tablets as we walked down the aisle. Row after row was full. *There must be two seats somewhere*, I thought. *They let us on the plane.* Then we saw an open middle seat. I let Hannah have that one and pushed onward. I found the other open seat way in the back. I sat down and looked at my watch: 5:50 a.m.

I found Hannah waiting for me when I walked off the plane at our connection in Dallas.

"How was the flight for you?" I asked.

"It was good. I made a friend," she said.

"Oh yeah?" I asked.

"Yeah, the lady I sat next to just moved to San Antonio with her husband and still works in Kansas City. That's where she was flying. Her name is Bliss. We're having dinner with her and her husband in two weeks," she said.

"Only you," I said, laughing and shaking my head.

We made it to Albuquerque and met up with a couple of friends coming in from other cities. The next morning, we all piled into the car well before dawn and headed to the hot air balloon festival. It was still dark when we got out of the car and walked through the crowded fairgrounds.

When we found our company's tent, we got a cup of coffee and a pre-flight safety briefing. It was our job not to get lost as we navigated through the masses of festival attendees to the deflated balloon. Once there, we would have to assist with the inflation process and then jump into the basket before ascension. The safety instructor emphasized the balloon could not wait for anyone who got lost in the crowd.

I knew nothing about hot air balloons and had not realized how much work and precision timing went into a successful lift-off. I started to feel a little stress about the unexpected job duties and tight schedule. Then, we met our pilot, who held multiple world records for air balloon travel. He explained balloons have no steering mechanism; the only thing the pilot controls is how high up or low the balloon goes. The wind blows in different directions at different altitudes, and balloon pilots ascend and descend into the different wind streams to head in their desired direction.

My anxiety started to climb. I wondered about the wisdom of getting in a floating balloon with no steering mechanism, world-record-holding pilot or not. What could the pilot do if the wind blew the wrong way? I looked over at Hannah; she was beaming with excitement. There was no backing out now.

I did not have much time to worry. The crew put us to work as soon as we met them at our balloon. While they blew air into the balloon with huge fans, we each held a rope tethered to the balloon's opening. Once it was inflated enough to be vertical, the pilot cut on the burner. It roared as it exhaled into the balloon. The festival workers backed the crowds away and told us to jump in the basket. We all jumped in.

Our pilot pulled the handle, and the burner roared louder. The basket lifted just a few inches off the ground, and my stomach flipped. The pilot's assistants put their backs against the basket and kept it steady. The pilot opened the burner to full blast. We lifted higher, and the assistants guided us forward until they could not reach the basket anymore. Then, we were off.

We floated upward and forward over a sea of people, vans, and grounded balloons as far as I could see. The sun was cresting the mountains to the east, rising with us. There were dozens of balloons ahead of us in the sky and hundreds more inflating on the ground behind us.

We climbed higher and higher until the pilot cut off the burner. The silence stunned me. I was accustomed to flying in planes with the sound of jet engines and the turbulence of wings being forced through the wind. The balloon could not have been more different. Floating in the hot air balloon thousands of feet above the ground is one of the quietest and stillest places I have ever been. Our pilot pointed out landmarks and occasionally lifted and lowered the balloon as we drifted in the direction he had planned before the flight.

When we started our descent, the pilot called to his ground crew from the radio. He had identified a landing spot and told his crew where to meet us. He lowered the balloon, then paused the descent a safe distance above some powerlines. The balloon behind us did not; it collided with the lines and fell to the ground.

I looked at the pilot and the ground below us. It was rising rapidly, and we were still flying forward fast, headed for a landing at an angle.

"My ground crew is not here," the pilot said. "Everyone hold on!"

The bottom of our basket hit the concrete, and we bounced back up into the air for a few seconds. Then we skipped off the concrete a few more times and went into a skid. We were headed for a sloped curb at the end of the road. We hit the curb, and our momentum carried us over into a dirt field. As we came to a stop in the dirt, the basket tilted over for a second, but then fell back onto the ground, right side up. Everyone in the basket burst into applause; we had landed.

I WILL BE honest—I am not in a rush to schedule another hot air balloon ride. Nevertheless, the trip to Albuquerque did teach me something about faith and fear.

Looking back, I realize I was never a fully committed atheist. Even at my most fervent, there was always one thing I could not explain—free will. An atheistic worldview, in which physical things are all that exist, leads to the philosophy of determinism, in which human actions are the inescapable consequences of prior events. In other words, a genuine atheistic worldview rejects the notion of free will.

I could never take that last step. Even as an atheist, I could not shake the feeling that I had free will. I could not adopt the bona fide atheist's position that the human experience of free will is just an elaborate, neurological illusion.

CHRISTIANITY EXPLAINS THAT FREE WILL IS A DIVINE GIFT.

Christianity explains that free will is a divine gift. It allows us to interact meaningfully rather than react automatically, to take part in—not just be a part of—the world.

The divine gift of free will comes with a catch. Our free will is infinite, but our abilities and sphere of control are limited. We get to choose our course, but we are not like commercial jets that fly against the wind with nothing but a bit of turbulence.

We are more like hot air balloons. Things happen to us, good and bad. Babies are born, promotions come, loved ones die, and companies go under. There are some winds in life we cannot fly against, but that does not mean we lose our free will.

In Albuquerque, I watched our pilot use the winds to steer a hot air balloon and land it in a vacant street, all without a ground crew. He did not succumb to fear and panic in the face of unfavorable conditions. He used his infinite free will to expand the finite limits of his control. Watching him operate, I learned we cannot control the wind, but we can control where it takes us.

On the way to Albuquerque, Hannah and I planned to sit together on our 6:00 a.m. flight, but that was not an option. Instead of being frustrated, Hannah reacted like a seasoned hot air balloon pilot, adjusting with the wind and letting it carry her forward. She could have popped in headphones and thought about how uncomfortable she was sitting next to strangers for fifty minutes, like I did. But she did not. Hannah did not see an inconvenience in the seat next to her; she saw a friend.

That is how Hannah met Bliss, a woman who was nervous about flying with her lap dog for the first time and was looking for friends in a new city. All these years later, Bliss and her husband, Kyle, are two of our closest friends. After my conversion to Christianity, Bliss was the first friend I got to witness choosing faith in Christ. Hannah and I did not preach to her over dinner. We just tried to be good friends and answered questions about our faith when asked. We rode the wind, and it carried us to Bliss's baptism four years to the month after the hot air balloon festival.

God's Word about Free Will:

✝ *Then God said, "Let us make mankind in our image, in our likeness, so that they may rule over the fish in the sea and the birds in the sky, over the livestock and all the wild animals, and over all the creatures that move along the ground."*

*So God created mankind in his own image,
in the image of God he created them;
male and female he created them.*

GENESIS 1:26–27 NIV

✝ *You, my brothers and sisters, were called to be free. But do not use your freedom to indulge the flesh; rather, serve one another humbly in love. For the entire law is fulfilled in keeping this one command: "Love your neighbor as yourself." If you bite and devour each other, watch out or you will be destroyed by each other.*

GALATIANS 5:13–15 NIV

✝ *Jesus answered, "My teaching is not my own. It comes from the one who sent me. Anyone who chooses to do the will of God will find out whether my teaching comes from God or whether I speak on my own. Whoever speaks on their own does so to gain personal glory, but he who seeks the glory of the one who sent him is a man of truth; there is nothing false about him."*

JOHN 7:16–18 NIV

Hey Pops —

    There are very few things in the world as special to me as going to a ballgame with you. I was honored to celebrate your birthday weekend with you and had a blast at the ballpark. I hope you enjoyed it at least half as much as I did.

    Birthdays tend to serve as reflection points. We measure our lives by our birthday and often think back and look ahead when the day comes around each year. I imagine this birthday felt different for you. Maybe you felt grateful to be alive at age 55 when many people never make it that long. Maybe you felt proud of the job you did providing for your family, as you realized both of your sons are well into their careers. Maybe you felt frustrated that this birthday came in the midst of taxing medical treatment. Maybe you felt a confident resolve to see many birthdays more; maybe you felt scared that you would not.

    Or maybe you felt all of these emotions and are looking for a way to make sense of everything. I know of only one fail-proof course of action in times of suffering: persevere through faith in Christ. In Romans 5:1-5, the apostle Paul wrote:

Therefore, since we have been justified through faith, we have peace with God through our Lord Jesus Christ, through whom we have gained access by faith into this grace in which we now stand. And we boast in the glory of God. Not only so, but we also glory in our sufferings, because we know that suffering produce perseverance; perseverance, character; and character, hope. And hope does not put us to shame, because God's love has been poured out into our hearts through the Holy Spirit, who has been given to us.

Our suffering in life is not meaningless; it is an opportunity to strengthen our spirit of hope. Everyone acknowledges suffering during training is a necessary ~~step~~ to become stronger and faster. As the saying attests, "No pain, no gain." Why should our spirit not be strengthened in the same way, by persevering through reps and sets of difficult days and weeks in times of suffering? But we must not try to persevere alone. The first line of the passage above emphasizes where our strength comes from by the source "through"

WHICH WE RECEIVE IT. WE CAN PERSEVERE THROUGH FAITH IN CHRIST AND THROUGH FAITH IN CHRIST ALONE.

WE WILL FIGHT TOGETHER;
TOGETHER, WE WILL WIN.
WITH A SON'S LOVE FOR
HIS FATHER,

CHAPTER FOURTEEN

Build Hope

June 28, 2020 – Kerrville, Texas

I FELT IT SHORTLY after the turn: the unforgettable knock of the most unwelcome visitor. A breeze started to rustle the leaves inside my head. *No, no, no*, I thought. I tried to shut my thoughts down and keep the door to my mind closed, but it was too late. I was having another panic attack.

I had been in the back of the pack from the start of the swim. I figured that would happen, since I had learned how to swim just five weeks before the race. I was confident in my plan and content with my slow and steady pace until everyone else was swimming past me on their way back from the halfway point. They were headed back to the ramp—back to dry ground—but I was still swimming out, moving farther from the finish line.

When I hit the halfway point and turned around, I was alone. I sighted forward on a breath. I could barely make out the arm stroke and splashes of the others far ahead of me. I stroked twice and reached my head to the right for a breath, but the wind slapped a small wave into my face and choked me. That is when fear came knocking. My thoughts spiraled in an instant, and anxiety started to ooze through my arteries. My heart pounded and my muscles trembled with excess nervous energy. I had half a mile left to get back to the ramp. Fear was telling me I would not make it.

FEAR DOES NOT care about style points; it likes to win. Once fear finds a winning strategy, it will run the same play over and over again. We call those plays "phobias." For other people, it may be heights, small spaces, or things that creep and crawl. But for me, it is water.

Water has terrified me since I was a kid. I learned to fear water when I was five years old. I was at the neighborhood pool, and another kid held me underwater. I felt like I was trapped below the surface for ages. I remember how everything looked blurry in the refracted sunlight as I panicked. I next encountered fear of water at the water park when I was twelve years old. I was in the deep end of the wave pool when my hamstring cramped. I remember my head bobbing above and below the surface as I fought to straighten out my cocked leg and swim back to where I could touch. By the time I was in high school, fear had me pinned. I could not swim in the backyard pool alone at night. It was a small pool; I was only a few strokes from the sides in every direction, but that did not matter. My fear of water was not rational, so it could not be reasoned away.

Fast forward to 2020, when Hannah and I decided to do a triathlon. I did not have to worry about the 13.1-mile run; training for my fifty-mile run would have me ready for that. The fifty-six-mile bike ride was long, but I immediately took to the bike and enjoyed getting out on the road. The 1.2-mile open-water swim was the big challenge for me, mostly because I did not know how to swim. I was not a drowning risk; I could tread water and make my way around a pool party. But I had never swum a lap or swum freestyle with my face in the water before.

My first training session at the pool started at 5:30 a.m. I sat on the edge and put my feet in. It was colder than I expected. I pushed myself off the edge, and the water passed over my waist and up to my shoulders. *Do people actually swim in this temperature?* I thought as my stomach tensed. I grabbed my swim cap and looked at it, trying to figure out which side was which. I put the front against my forehead and pulled it back over my head. But it was only covering three-quarters of my hair. The rest of the cap was bunched up in loose slack on the top of my head. I grabbed the right side of the cap and pulled it down and away from my head as far as I could to stretch it out, but my wet fingers slipped from the latex. WHAP! The swim cap slapped me across the ear. I cursed as my ear rang. The swim cap knew I had no idea what I was doing. It was trying to wake me up, to prepare me for the suffering.

I put my goggles on and did a few of those arm stretches Olympic swimmers always do. *Well, here we go*, I thought. I started my watch and pushed off from the side of the pool. I made it about eight strokes before I realized I needed to breathe. I stopped my arm strokes and craned my entire head out of the water. I took a long, noisy breath, then plunged my head back in and started stroking again.

Four strokes later, I had to repeat the process. *How long is this pool?* I thought as I came up for my third breath. When I made it to the other end of the pool, I stood up, turned around, and looked back at the distance I had covered. My heart was pounding, my legs were burning, and I was doing mental math. *That was twenty-five meters. I have to do eight hundred meters today, which means I have to do that thirty-one more times. There is no way!*

I pushed off and headed back down the pool. When I paused to come up for air, my lower body sank. I lost all momentum and then started stroking again. My legs were on fire, burning up all my oxygen. Every few seconds I sucked air like someone who had been trapped in a sinking car for two minutes. I stood up when I hit the wall. *Fifty meters. Thirty laps left.*

I kept fighting my way across the pool, twenty-five meters at a time. On most laps, I had to stop and stand somewhere in the middle for a few seconds. I was going to try to swim 1.2 miles in open water, but I could not make it twenty-five meters across a pool. When I was halfway done with the workout, I stopped for a break at the end of my lane and watched Hannah in the lane next to me. She looked effortless, like she was gliding across the surface of the water. She touched the wall and stopped for a quick rest next to me.

"I'm really struggling. I must be doing something wrong," I said.

"Can you show me?" she asked. I pushed away from the wall and swam about twenty feet, then turned around and came back.

"Why are you doing your legs like that?" she asked.

"Like what?"

"You're frog kicking your legs out all wild. You are going like this," she said and pushed off from the side. I watched as her legs darted around underwater. *I'm not doing that*, I said to myself. But as soon as I saw her, I knew she was right. As I watched her legs, I could feel mine burning.

Realizing I was kicking my legs like a frog in a frying pan was only 10 percent of the battle for me. I was embarrassed my body awareness in the pool was so poor I did not know I was frog kicking. But I was more embarrassed that my coordination in the pool was so poor I could not stop doing it even after I realized it. No matter how hard I tried, my legs flailed uncontrollably in the water. Every time I craned my head out of the water to breathe, my legs started to sink. My legs did not like this, so they churned harder to push back to the surface, which burned more oxygen and made me more desperate for air. It was a vicious, dysfunctional cycle.

I finished that first swim workout in record slow time. Multiple swimmers entered the pool, got a full workout in, and left during my 800-meter effort. After I had showered, changed, and driven to the office, I was at my desk, wondering how I would ever be able to swim 1.2 miles. Then, without the courtesy of a warning, an ounce of chlorinated water poured out from my nose onto the keyboard in front of me. *Seriously?*

I suffered through months of miserable 5:30 a.m. swims full of choking, gasping, leg flailing, and post-swim nose leaking. I spent hours watching videos online about form and drills. I read articles debating whether I should use the two-count, four-count, or six-count kick. I practiced coordinating the movement of my arms and legs on the floor of my bedroom.

Over the course of a few months, I improved my breathing, body rotation, and arm strokes, but the kick still evaded me. Each day when I got into the pool, I hoped it would be the day I finally got it. Each day, the same thing happened: I could not control my kicking, so I burned up all my oxygen and had to stop every twenty-five meters.

Five weeks before the 1.2-mile swim, I still could not swim more than fifty meters without stopping. I had tried every drill and trick available online, but nothing worked. I was lamenting after a bike ride one day when my friend George offered a solution so simple it shocked me.

"Don't kick," he said.

"But my legs will sink," I told him.

"That's okay. You can swim like that. Use a buoy at first to help you get used to it. Just don't kick."

I was skeptical of the plan. I knew my legs were dense and would sink like an anchor. But with five weeks until the swim, I was running out of options. When I got into the pool the next time, I stuck a buoy between my legs and pushed off from the wall. My pace was slow as my legs sank and dragged behind me. I focused on relaxing them, on being okay with the sinking, on being okay with swimming slowly. My legs wanted to panic and churn when they sank, but I did not let them.

I surprised myself when I hit the fifty-meter mark. I was tired, but I was not gasping for air. I pushed off the wall for another lap. *Relax. Stay loose. Don't fight the water.* I talked to myself the entire way down the pool. My breathing fell into a rhythm. Each time I turned my head for a breath, I blew a small puff of air out my nose to clear water out of the way before I inhaled. When I hit the 100-meter mark, I was shocked. I pushed off the wall for another lap. I did not have to focus as much on my legs. They were powered down and loose behind me. My heart rate felt steady. I was in the zone.

I swam 800 meters that day without stopping. I was not fast. I had not figured out the secret trick to kicking or swimming on the surface. But I learned something more valuable—I learned how to be okay being uncomfortable in the water. That lesson saved me on race day five weeks later.

When my anxiety cranked up after the turnaround point, I did not let it ruin my race. I slowed down and called out to my friend on the kayak, who turned around and paddled out to me. I held onto the kayak for a few deep breaths, then nodded to my friend and started swimming again. It was a long half-mile swim back to the ramp, my form was poor, and I was in last place in our makeshift triathlon. But I did not let being tired, slow, or half-sunken under water stop me. I swam through the suffering.

A CRASH COURSE in learning to swim taught me an important lesson: suffering helps growth. I suffered physically, mentally, and emotionally in the pool. I was cold, tired, out of breath, frustrated, and embarrassed. I hated choking on water and struggling to make it twenty-five meters when everyone else was gliding around.

But I did not stop. I kept working. Swimming through suffering gave me perseverance, character, and hope. It taught me I was not limited to the point where suffering started. I could keep going, and I would be better for it.

SUFFERING BUILDS HOPE, AND HOPE CRUSHES FEAR.

Fear wants us to be afraid of suffering. It wants us to withdraw and refrain from any action that might cause us to suffer. Why? Because when we work through suffering rather than hiding from it, we develop perseverance, character, and hope. Suffering builds hope, and hope crushes fear. Hope is the ultimate product of suffering, and hope is exactly what people who are suffering need most.

I do not want anyone to have cancer, go through a divorce, or lose a child. And I do not believe God wants those things either. But we live in a fallen world where bad things happen. If we spend all our days obsessed with avoiding any suffering, however small, our hope muscles will be severely underdeveloped when a real tragedy strikes and we need them. Hope is real, but it is not a gratuitous product of wishful thinking. We have to build it.

GOD'S WORD ABOUT HOPE:

✝ *Therefore, since we have been justified through faith, we have peace with God through our Lord Jesus Christ, through whom we have gained access by faith into this grace in which we now stand. And we boast in the hope of the glory of God. Not only so, but we also glory in our sufferings, because we know that suffering produces perseverance; perseverance, character; and character, hope. And hope does not put us to shame, because God's love has been poured out into our hearts through the Holy Spirit, who has been given to us.*

ROMANS 5:1–5 NIV

✝ *I remember my affliction and my wandering,*
the bitterness and the gall.
I well remember them,
and my soul is downcast within me.
Yet this I call to mind
and therefore I have hope:
Because of the LORD's great love we are not consumed,
for his compassions never fail.
They are new every morning;
great is your faithfulness.
I say to myself, "The LORD is my portion;
therefore I will wait for him."
The LORD is good to those whose hope is in him,
to the one who seeks him;
it is good to wait quietly
for the salvation of the LORD.

LAMENTATIONS 3:19–26 NIV

✟ *Let us hold unswervingly to the hope we profess, for he who promised is faithful. And let us consider how we may spur one another on toward love and good deeds, not giving up meeting together, as some are in the habit of doing, but encouraging one another—and all the more as you see the Day approaching.*

HEBREWS 10:23–25 NIV

Hey Pops —

Have you ever felt overwhelmed by what you do not know? I sometimes feel as though I am in a kayak trying to paddle my way over every square inch of ocean. The further I go, the more I realize how little I have covered. This feeling can be disheartening, especially in times of unwelcome change and trial, when we have less certainty still. If I am in a kayak at sea, perhaps you feel you are treading water, with neither land nor boat in sight.

It is at these times, when we are most likely to concentrate on the pragmatic and utilitarian, that it is most critical for us to appreciate the beautiful. Beauty is one of the most powerful proofs of God's existence. When we hear the soft cry of the violin hovering over the orchestra, it moves us. When we see the sun dip into the water, casting streams of pink and orange above the salty air, it stops us. These experiences mean something. The reality of beauty, the meaning that transcends the mere grouping and sequence of sounds and colors, is to me self-evident. Bach's Air on a G String is not equal to any random cacophony;

IT IS BEAUTY. IT IS A FLEETING GLIMPSE OF THE IMMUTABLE CHARACTERISTIC OF THE COMING WORLD REDEEMED BY CHRIST.

IN ROMANS 1:20, THE APOSTLE PAUL WROTE:

> FOR EVER SINCE THE WORLD WAS CREATED, PEOPLE HAVE SEEN THE EARTH AND SKY. THROUGH EVERYTHING GOD MADE, THEY CAN CLEARLY SEE HIS INVISIBLE QUALITIES — HIS ETERNAL POWER AND DIVINE NATURE. SO THEY HAVE NO EXCUSE FOR NOT KNOWING GOD.

WHEN WE PERCEIVE BEAUTY IN THE WORLD, WE ARE WITNESSING SOMETHING BEYOND MERE VIBRATIONS AND MOLECULES; WE ARE WITNESSING GOD. IN ONE OF MY DARKEST HOURS AS AN ATHIEST, I GOT A TATTOO THAT, WHEN TRANSLATED FROM SPANISH TO ENGLISH, READS, "EACH DAY HAS BEAUTY; MAKE YOUR OWN HAPPINESS." I KNEW THERE WAS SOMETHING SIGNIFICANT ABOUT BEAUTY, BUT COULD NOT APPRECIATE IT AS ANYTHING MORE THAN A TOOL. I REALIZE NOW THAT BEAUTY IS MUCH MORE THAN A TOOL. IT IS EVIDENCE. IT IS FORESHADOWING. IT IS OUR PURPOSE AND GOD'S PROMISE.

THERE IS BEAUTY EVERYWHERE, POPS, EVEN IN HOSPITAL HALLS AND WAITING

ROOMS. DON'T PASS THE OPPORTUNITY
TO APPRECIATE IT.

WE WILL FIGHT TOGETHER;
TOGETHER, WE WILL WIN.
WITH A SON'S LOVE FOR
HIS FATHER,

CHAPTER FIFTEEN

Spot Beauty

April 19, 2019 – Espiritu Santo Bay, Texas

I PADDLED MY KAYAK over to a cut in the sea grass. I wanted to try one last spot before heading back to the dock empty-handed. I glided on the surface of the shallow bay. Signs of life appeared as the water churned around my kayak. *I found the honey hole!*

I put a red, soft plastic lure on the end of my line and cast it out. It must have been my thousandth cast since I had last caught a fish. I reeled, paused, and reeled some more. Then I felt it: the unforgettable but increasingly unfamiliar bump on the other end of the line. I pulled back to set the hook and started to reel in the prize for my patience and perseverance. The thrill of the catch was coursing in my blood again.

But as I reeled my line, the thrill faded into confusion. Something felt off. I did not feel the fight of a fish in my rod. Nor did I feel the dead weight of being snagged on a rock or root. Whatever was on the other end of my line was light but alive. It was moving a lot but not exerting much force. I reeled the end of my line to within a few feet of my kayak, lifted my rod, and raised my mystery catch from the murky water. *What in the world?*

THEY SAY PEOPLE enjoy what they are good at. I have a counterexample: I enjoy fishing. Hannah and I own several fishing poles, two boxes of tackle, aerated buckets for live bait, two kayaks, and a cooler full of other fishing tools. For as much gear as I have acquired and all the times I have gone fishing, I have an embarrassing secret. I have never caught a saltwater keeper.

A keeper is a fish bigger than the minimum size required by the state to keep a fish of that species. If your fish is smaller than the limit, you have to release it. For whatever reason, the hooks on the end of my line attract fish one inch shorter than the limit. But I remain confident I will catch my saltwater keeper one day. And when I do, it is going to be a world record. It will be the most expensive fish ever caught. When you add up all the money I have spent on gear, live bait, and fuel to get to the coast, then divide that number by one fish, you get a really big number. Every bite of that fish will be worth thousands of dollars.

Catching fish is not the main reason I enjoy fishing. If it were, I would go fishing much less. My favorite thing about fishing is beauty—the beauty when I push my kayak out from the dock into the twilight and watch the sun rise over the water, the beauty when I am alone with the wind, drifting silently over the shallow bay, the beauty when the sea life forgets I am there and relaxes, when stingrays glide underneath me and sea turtles poke their heads up for a breath.

The ocean's beauty is what kept me going through a particularly rough fishing season a few years ago. It started in the winter, when my fishing buddy, Brien, and I loaded our kayaks and headed to the coast. We fished for more than six hours without a single bite.

"The water is still too cold. We'll get them next time," I said as we drove back.

I had no idea what I was talking about, but it seemed like a reasonable explanation. Next time brought the same results: absolutely nothing. After another unsuccessful trip, I was starting to think I was cursed. Even the people with me could not get a bite. I planned one more day trip to the coast, convinced I could not possibly strike out again.

"I've got a good feeling about today," I announced that morning as Hannah and I launched our kayaks.

We bought some live bait and paddled out to meet up with Brien and his wife, Lizzie. We fished the shallow bay, the shoreline, and the surf. We fished with live bait and with artificial lures. Nothing.

By the afternoon, the sun was high, and morale was low. Hannah and Lizzie had paddled over to a bank hours earlier to talk and rest. Brien could fish all day, but even he was getting worn out by the lack of action. I paddled away from the group and across the main channel to another cut we had not tried. I wanted to test one more spot.

I turned the corner and glided over a shallow grassy area. The water stirred around my kayak. Signs of life. I put the red, soft plastic lure on my line, and cast out. I felt the unforgettable bump on my line and set the hook. I reeled the end of my line to within a few feet of my kayak, lifted my rod, and raised my catch from the water.

A crab the size of my hand was dangling in front of me with the hook of my lure pierced through its right arm. I froze as the crab flailed around in mid-air, searching for a solution to its predicament. Five or ten seconds that felt like an hour passed by, and I did not move. Then, the crab stopped flailing, locked its beady black eyes on mine, reached its left claw up … and snipped its right arm off. The crab plopped back into the water and left its right arm dangling from my line, swaying in the wind. I sat in my kayak, speechless.

As symbolic as the encounter felt, I have no idea what it meant. I do not know anyone else who has speared a crab in the arm while fishing with an artificial lure, much less watched it escape by self-amputation. Just when I thought I was figuring out a small sliver of the ocean, it gave me something I never expected.

That is what makes the ocean both the most beautiful and frightening part of the world to me. I go out of my way to spend time by and on the ocean everywhere I travel, yet nothing can crank my fear alarm up like the thought of being swept out to sea.

The ocean has the traits necessary to inspire and overwhelm. It is endless. Like a star-filled sky on a clear night, you cannot take it all in at one moment. It is a calm tide pool on a white sand beach in the tropics, frigid ten-foot waves crashing into the ice of Antarctica, and dense darkness miles below the surface.

Its power and patience are limitless. It can swallow massive ships in an instant and cut through solid rock one splash at a time.

And it holds countless mysteries. If I lived a thousand years and dedicated my life to studying the ocean, I would never see it all or learn a tenth of its secrets.

FROM THE PERSPECTIVE of one human life, the ocean is infinite. That is what makes it both more beautiful and more frightening than smaller bodies of water, like ponds. The finite becomes less beautiful the more we experience it, but the infinite, though it may be intimidating, becomes more beautiful. The infinite never grows stale or becomes tamed. We never get it mapped out. The infinite always contains unknowns, but what makes the unknown frightening also makes it beautiful.

THE INFINITE ALWAYS CONTAINS UNKNOWNS, BUT WHAT MAKES THE UNKNOWN FRIGHTENING ALSO MAKES IT BEAUTIFUL.

I am grateful God gives us a life more like the infinite ocean than a pond. We do not have a curated short list of options and experiences—we do not have to sit on the same dock and cast into the same pond for the same fish day after day. We have a vast expanse to explore with our free will. Each day brings the opportunity to embark upon new adventures with new people, and there is beauty in that journey.

A life like a pond might be safer—without things like storms, currents, and sea creatures to worry about—but would it be better? I wish terrible things like cancer did not happen. But I do not wish for a world like a pond, where the removal of danger is possible only if we live in a limited and lackluster environment. Instead, I wish for the world I glimpse in the moments of beauty I spot—the world redeemed by God that lies ahead of us.

God's Word about Beauty:

✝ *For ever since the world was created, people have seen the earth and sky. Through everything God made, they can clearly see his invisible qualities – his eternal power and divine nature. So they have no excuse for not knowing God.*

Romans 1:20 NLT

✝ *Where can I go from your Spirit?*
Where can I flee from your presence?
If I go up to the heavens, you are there;
if I make my bed in the depths, you are there.
If I rise on the wings of the dawn,
if I settle on the far side of the sea,
even there your hand will guide me,
your right hand will hold me fast.
If I say, "Surely the darkness will hide me
and the light become night around me,"
even the darkness will not be dark to you;
the night will shine like the day,
for darkness is as light to you.

For you created my inmost being;
you knit me together in my mother's womb.
I praise you because I am fearfully and wonderfully made;
your works are wonderful,
I know that full well.
My frame was not hidden from you
when I was made in the secret place,
when I was woven together in the depths of the earth.
Your eyes saw my unformed body;
all the days ordained for me were written in your book
before one of them came to be.
How precious to me are your thoughts, God!
How vast is the sum of them!
Were I to count them,
they would outnumber the grains of sand—
when I awake, I am still with you.

PSALM 139:7–18 NIV

✝ *Finally, brothers and sisters, whatever is true, whatever is noble, whatever is right, whatever is pure, whatever is lovely, whatever is admirable—if anything is excellent or praiseworthy—think about such things.*

PHILIPPIANS 4:8 NIV

Hey Pops —

It's here: the last week of Phase one of your treatment. It seems like the weeks have flown by to me; I'm sure you feel different. I want you to know how proud I am of your courage and how impressed I am by your strength. In your season of trial, you are carrying your cross with both hope and humility. You are not just surviving, you are thriving. Yet again you are teaching me how to be a great man, not by your words alone, but by your actions.

As you approach this milestone of your journey, ~~there is a p~~ I encourage you to reflect on God's promise to those in pain. God has a message for the sick and the crippled, the depressed and the destitute, the exhausted and the grieving. In Isaiah 40:29-31, the prophet wrote:

> Even youths grow tired and weary,
> and young men stumble and fall;
> But those who hope in the Lord
> will renew their strength.
> They will soar on wings like eagles;
> They will run and not grow weary,
> They will walk and not be faint.

When this treatment regimen feels like more than you can bear, focus on the eternal future free of pain and exhaustion. These words are probably easier for me to write than they are for you to read. I may not be able to comprehend the full physical and mental toll of your diagnosis and treatment, but how much less can we comprehend the gift of renewed life? No matter how the scene or act is playing out right now, our story is not a tragedy. It is a story with the greatest, most joyous ending possible: an ending that is not an ending, but a being full of glory beyond our comprehension.

I hope this reality brings you peace and joy, right here and right now. And remember, Pops, that you are never alone.

We will fight together; together, we will win. With a son's love for his father,

Renew Strength

July 4, 2019 – Amalfi Coast, Italy

T HE SUN BEAT down on us as we walked along the shadeless, rocky cliff. *I'm from Texas; I'm not supposed to be hot in Italy*, I thought as I took another swig of water. The sweat dripping from my chin disagreed. I patted my hand against the pocket of my pack where I would normally carry snacks. Still empty. *We should have come across the restaurant by now*, I thought. But all I could see ahead were more rocks.

HANNAH AND I took a trip to the Amalfi Coast of Italy a few weeks before my father's cancer diagnosis. While we were planning it, I read about a hike called the Path of the Gods. "It's just an hour-and-a-half hike and only a few miles from where we are staying," I told her. I did not mention the recommendation I had read about avoiding the hike during the summer months.

"Oh, that's right by a restaurant I want to go to," she said as she looked at the map on my laptop.

We typed "hike and lunch" into our itinerary. We had no idea what we signed up for.

We stayed in Positano, a beautiful collage of colorful homes built into the cliff above the Mediterranean Sea. The lodging in Positano is more affordable with each stair you climb. After paying for the flights and all the fun things we wanted to do, Hannah and I decided to rest our bank account at the expense of our legs when it came to lodging. We stayed in a tiny room at the top of the city, several hundred steep stone steps above the sea.

The morning of the hike we ate breakfast, loaded our packs with water, and started the thirty-minute walk down from our hotel to the Positano dock. I did not bother packing food. Hannah's restaurant near the end of the hike was supposed to be amazing, and I did not want to spoil my appetite with trail mix. When we got to the dock at the city center, we boarded a crowded ferry for a half-hour ride up the coast to the town of Amalfi. We got off the ferry in Amalfi and were still a few miles from the start of the hiking trail. Dozens of taxis lined the street outside the ferry stop. All the sedan-style taxis looked like they had come off the assembly line before I was born. The white, van-style taxis were more vehicle than two people needed, but they looked to be in a lot better shape. I picked the newest-looking one.

"We want to go to the start of the Path of the Gods trail," I told the driver.

"Yes," he said in a thick accent. I was not sure he had understood me, but I decided to trust him. I negotiated what was probably a grossly expensive fare, and then Hannah and I hopped in. We buckled our seat belts just before the van shot forward into the busy street. I clenched the armrests and looked over at Hannah. Her eyes widened.

Our driver raced up the cliff. The van listed left and right as we whipped around the hairpin, switchback turns. Our side mirrors were within an inch of the cliff wall on one side and oncoming traffic on the other. I grabbed the Dramamine we had packed for the ferry ride and took one. Then, just when I thought I could not ride any further, the van snapped to a stop.

"Here," the driver said. I handed him the euros and jumped out of the van. I turned around to help Hannah out and shut the door behind her. The driver took off.

"Where are we?" Hannah asked.

"I don't know," I answered as I looked around. I had been so thankful to get out of the van I had not bothered checking where we were. It looked like an abandoned town. There were stone buildings everywhere, but no people. We wandered a little further down the street and found a tiny café with the door propped open. We peeked inside; there were no patrons. We shrugged at each other, walked in, and ordered coffees from the family working there.

"We are looking for the Path of the Gods," I told the woman working behind the counter after I paid. She stared back at me. I tried again in fragments of broken Italian. The woman pointed out the window to her left. It was not much, but it would have to do.

Hannah and I knocked back our coffees and took a left out of the café. We walked down a narrow, empty alley for a few hundred feet. We weaved between old houses as we followed the alley further and further from town. We still had not seen another tourist or hiker since we exited the white van. *This can't be right*, I thought to myself. *We are going to get lost before we even start the hike.* Then, the alley turned right and formed a short bridge over a valley, and we saw a small sign with an arrow that read, "Sentiero degli Dei"—the Path of the Gods.

We crossed the bridge and came to a fork: left or up a flight of stairs. We chose left, which was wrong. We doubled back a few minutes later after hitting a dead end. We took the stairs and found another small Sentiero degli Dei sign and followed it. After another ten minutes of walking, and more than two hours after we left our hotel room, we finally found it: the big Sentiero degli Dei sign—the start of the trail. I was relieved we had found the trailhead, but nervous about how much of the cool morning had passed before we had even started. After about a mile, I realized my concern was justified.

The hike started out pleasantly as we walked along terraced land in the shade of the surrounding cliffs. We crossed paths and exchanged smiles with dozens of other hikers traversing the trail in the opposite direction. At one point, the trail took us across a shaded stream with hundreds of cairns lining its wide bank. The shade did not last.

The trail climbed out from the safe harbor of the trees after about a mile and started a long and winding journey along the top of the cliff. The views of the sea below us were breathtaking, but there was nothing between us and the mid-day July sun. We hit another fork without a sign. Left was wrong last time, so this time we chose to go right. We walked uphill about a quarter mile before running into a dead end at the house of a confused-looking man working in his garden. Wrong again. We doubled back to the fork and took the left path.

As the sun grew more intense, we stopped crossing other hikers. Everyone else headed in the opposite direction had started much earlier. It was after 2:00 p.m. when we finally arrived at the little town on the other end of the Path of the Gods. Between the walk down from our hotel room to the dock, the ferry, the taxi, the hike to start the hike, the two wrong turns, and the Path of Gods itself, we were nearly five hours into our hour-and-a-half hike. My stomach felt empty, and my legs felt heavy. I was relieved to be at our destination and ready to eat something, anything! We walked down a few of the alleys in the tiny town, looking for Hannah's restaurant.

"I don't think the restaurant is in this town. It must be further," she said.

"Let's just grab something to eat here," I said as my stomach growled.

"I really want to go to the restaurant I found," she said.

I closed my eyes, hung my head, and hiked onward. There was no more trail. We were walking down a long winding road in what I hoped was the general direction of Positano. I longed to see the restaurant each time we rounded a corner, but all I found was a fresh stretch of road to walk. After about a dozen disappointments, it finally happened. We turned a corner and saw Hannah's restaurant.

It was built into the side of the cliff overlooking the Mediterranean. From the road, the hostess walked us through the restaurant's garden and across the dining room to a table for two. The seaward-facing wall of the restaurant was open with white linen curtains tied off and swaying in the cool breeze. We could see yachts and sailboats hundreds of feet below carving white, foamy lines in the blue, sparkling water. I sat in a daze of hunger and awe.

"I told you!" Hannah said, beaming at me.

Our waiter approached and asked us a single question: "Red wine or white wine?" It was the only question he asked all afternoon. After he brought us a bottle of wine and poured our glasses, he started bringing food to the table, no ordering necessary. First up was an antipasto tray of roasted vegetables and cheese. Next, he brought a plate loaded with four different types of pasta. I thought the meal was over after that, but our waiter then brought us a platter with an assortment of grilled meats. And, of course, he brought us a homemade dessert and two limoncellos to finish it off. We had no idea what was coming next at any given point, and we loved it! We ate a four-course meal without saying anything to our waiter other than "Thank you," over and over again.

As I ate, looked out over the sea, and shared the beauty of the moment with the person I most love to share beautiful moments with, my energy returned. My mental clarity grew, and I thought about the journey that had led us there. *The views really were fantastic; they were unlike anything I have ever seen. It was hot, no doubt, but it was not that bad.* The more my strength was renewed, the more beautiful the hike seemed, as if I could not see the hike for what it was until I was at the end.

"I think this is what Heaven is like," Hannah mused, as she looked out over the sea.

I smiled. I agreed. Not because I think Heaven is a four-course lunch with Hannah overlooking the Mediterranean, although that does sound lovely. I do not know what Heaven will look like, but that does not scare me. I think Heaven will be like the lunch at Hannah's restaurant because we will receive exactly what we need, whether we know what that is or not. I am not worried about what is on the menu because I do not have to order. God promises to give us not what we want but what we need: renewed strength. And when that happens, the walks of our lives will look different. The beautiful will appear more beautiful, and painful will feel less painful. In Heaven, we will see fear for the thin lie it always was.

> GOD PROMISES TO GIVE US NOT WHAT WE WANT BUT WHAT WE NEED: RENEWED STRENGTH.

Hannah and I left the restaurant renewed and reenergized. We hiked down the cliffside to Positano and then up the long stairs to our room in high spirits and smiles. The lunch was more than just calories for metabolic fuel. It was one of those moments when you can feel God's presence in the world: one of those moments when, despite the chaos and tragedies we all experience, you know the world is meaningful and good.

I am thankful to God for all those moments, but I am especially grateful for the magical lunch with Hannah on the cliffside of the Path of the Gods. While I did not know it in the moment, it was the touch of God I needed to strengthen me for what came next. The same month we returned from Italy, my father called me to tell me he had esophageal cancer.

GOD'S WORD ABOUT RENEWAL:

✝ *Even youths grow tired and weary,*
and young men stumble and fall;
but those who hope in the LORD
will renew their strength.
They will soar on wings like eagles;
they will run and not grow weary,
they will walk and not be faint.

ISAIAH 40:30–31 NIV

✝ *Therefore we do not lose heart. Though outwardly we are*
wasting away, yet inwardly we are being renewed day by
day. For our light and momentary troubles are achieving
for us an eternal glory that far outweighs them all. So we
fix our eyes not on what is seen, but on what is unseen, since
what is seen is temporary, but what is unseen is eternal.

2 CORINTHIANS 4:16–18 NIV

✝ *Trust in the LORD with all your heart*
and lean not on your own understanding;
in all your ways submit to him,
and he will make your paths straight.

PROVERBS 3:5–6 NIV

October 7, 2019

Hey Pops —   1/2

        It was one of the highest honors
of my life to be at your side when
you rang the bell to celebrate your
completion of phase one of treatment.
The sound of the bell was still
echoing in my head hours later on my
flight home. I thought of the bells in
treatment centers around the world. They
are audible celebrations of hope in
places where the enemy is trying to
spread despair. It was not every week
that someone rang the bell. Some weeks the
room was full of sick people with
weeks and months of treatment ahead of
them. This ~~does~~ does not deter the bells.
They wait in patient obedience and excited
anticipation for the next day they are
called upon to sing. The bells are more
than musical instruments. They are a
symbol of the spirit of the patient's
perseverance; they are a symbol of the
hope we have through Christ.
        As you move into the next phase
of treatment and prepare for surgery,
I hope you will remember the sound
of the bell. The bell never doubted
the day would come when you would ring
it for all to hear. The bell has no

Doubt you will be ringing it on the other side of your surgery.

I wrote the following poem on my flight home after your last treatment, on the day you rang the bell.

<u>Bells</u>

They do not despair in the silence
Or lose faith in the song to be sung;
Do not hold their tongues in defiance,
But hope everyday to be rung.
They are not deterred by the darkness
Or worried of not being found;
Do not slump or give up their hardness,
But stay flexed tight and ready to sound.
They do not covet the violin's strings
Or boast of their voices in pride;
Do not sing only for princes or kings,
But for the broken and those cast aside.

I cannot wait to hear you ring the bell again.

We will fight together;
Together, we will win.
With a son's love for
his father,

CHAPTER SEVENTEEN

Give Gifts

Winter 2020 – San Antonio, Texas

I LOOKED AT THE brown, leather journal on my desk. I picked up the bell sitting on top of it, set it on my desk, and grabbed the journal. I held it in both hands and ran my thumbs over the letters of the poem embossed on the front cover. I pulled the elastic band down, opened the journal, and flipped through the thick, cream-colored pages. They were blank, just as they had been all the times before.

MY TWO MOST prized possessions are gifts. One is the bell my father rang when he finished the first phase of his cancer treatment. It is customary for cancer patients to ring a bell when they complete a treatment regimen. Most chemo and radiation facilities have a bell mounted on the wall or set out on the counter for this purpose.

My friend Sarah gifted me a metal cowbell with a metal clapper during my father's treatment. It is no flimsy bell. It is a well-built noise-making machine. I carried it with me when I flew to Atlanta for my father's final round of chemotherapy. The bells he rang at the chemo and radiation centers were special, but they could not compare to the sheer celebratory volume of the cowbell. I stood by my father's side when he rang the cowbell on the afternoon of his last chemo and radiation treatment. It echoed through the apartment and still echoes in my memory.

Sarah is the best gift-giver I have ever known. I have seen her give gifts so thoughtful, special, and well-timed that the entire room, not just the recipient, was moved to tears. If the award for best gift-giver goes to Sarah, the award for second place goes to my father. He transformed into a different person and radiated with giddy enthusiasm every Christmas when I was a child. And he did not stop as I grew older.

One Christmas, when I was twenty-eight years old, he showered me with gifts, including the second of my two most prized possessions: a leather-bound journal with a poem embossed on the front cover. I was caught off guard by the gift because I did not think my father had ever read a poem before.

"This is a very nice journal, son," he said as he rubbed the leather and flipped through the thick pages. "Successful attorneys like you should have nice journals like this. It will look good on your desk."

"Thanks, Pops," I said as I took it. Some people may think my father's sentiment was superficial, but I do not. I did not care that my father had not read the poem. He gifted me the journal because he thought I was amazing, wanted me to know he thought I was amazing, and wanted me to have the things he thought amazing people should have.

It is astonishing to me how God unites people with different interests at beautiful intersections. My father, whose reading materials consisted of sales reports and restaurant menus, gifted me, the English major, my favorite poem. I had never read it before I received the journal that Christmas. I had heard people quote one of the lines, "not all those who wander are lost," but had never read the full poem.

It is by J.R.R. Tolkien, in the first book of his classic trilogy, *The Lord of the Rings*:

> *All that is gold does not glitter,*
> *not all those who wander are lost;*
> *the old that is strong does not wither,*
> *deep roots are not reached by the frost.*
> *From the ashes a fire shall be woken,*
> *a light from the shadows shall spring;*
> *renewed shall be blade that was broken,*
> *the crownless again shall be king.*[2]

As part of a novel, the poem has a context: it regards a specific character and literal sword at a given point in the story arc. But to me, the poem goes much deeper than that. The poem is the most beautiful description of Christ I have ever read.

---

[2] J.R.R. Tolkien, *The Fellowship of the Ring* (New York: HarperCollins, 2007), 170.

Christ did not come into the world glittered in jewels or regal robes, but as the son of a carpenter in a remote village. Because of Christ, no matter how far we wander from God, we are not lost. God's love expressed through Christ is the revelation of the old and strong, the infinite and all-powerful God, whose roots are so deep the whole word is built upon them.

Even the coldest, longest, darkest winter did not wither Christ; He was frost-bitten but stayed rooted in God. Like Christ, when our situation seems most dire—when we are diagnosed with a terminal illness, when we are wrongfully imprisoned for life, when a loved one dies—we are a pile of torched ashes in the darkness.

But look, there is a spark and now a fire growing from our ashes; light is conquering darkness. Christ is the sword broken against our sins and the King who gave up His crown to save us. He was raised from the dead, the sword mended, and crown restored. If we grasp onto Him, Christ the King, no matter how dark and deep our valley, we are lifted, mended, and restored in light.

This is the message I read in Tolkien's poem. It is the message of Christian hope, the ultimate story of conquering fear. It is victory through apparent defeat and restoration through apparent destruction. The fire and light of new life emerge from the ashes of our fallen life. There are no hopeless places or lost people; there is kindling with which to build a fire.

What made Jesus brave enough to be the blade that was broken? What gave Him the courage to bear His literal cross and endure the crucifixion? I think these are important questions for us to ask. If we are called to follow Him and bear our metaphorical crosses, we should seek what helped Jesus conquer fear. There may be many answers, but I think one is that He was giving us a gift. The more we focus on giving to someone else, the less of a grip fear has over us.

I like that my two most prized possessions are gifts, and I think God does, too. I can buy myself a lot of things in life, but I cannot buy myself a gift. I can buy something for myself and put a bow on it. I can even write myself a card. But I cannot buy myself the love that makes a chunk of metal, some leather, and sheets of paper into the two most special items I own.

Christianity is the same way; it is all about the beauty of gifts given in love. God gifted us an existence in His beautiful creation, then gifted us salvation after we fell. Christianity is an invitation to join an infinite gift exchange. We are all invited: you, me, my father, and everyone else we have ever met.

The bell my father rang sits on top of the journal he gave me, both next to me on the desk as I write this. I did not write in the journal for a long time. I picked it up, opened it, and flipped through the empty pages many times. It seemed too important for grocery lists or attorney notes. I thought about using it for poetry or new writing ideas, but the thought of tarnishing the perfect, clean pages with my words repulsed me.

Then, one day, I was reading about the power of writing down our dreams, and it clicked. I looked at the bell sitting on top of the leather journal. I remembered everything the bell stood for: my father's courage, the love in a gift from a friend, the joy of renewed life. I grabbed the journal from under the bell and started writing.

I wrote everything I want to do in my life. Some things, like playing guitar for a Bruce Springsteen cover band, are far off, while others, like writing this book, are closer at hand. But I wrote everything I could think of, as fast as I could. I did not want fear to censor me. I did not want to spend one more day doing anything less than making the most of the gifts God has given me.

GOD'S WORD ABOUT GIFTS:

✝ *For it is by grace you have been saved, through faith—and this is not from yourselves, it is the gift of God—not by works, so that no one can boast.*

EPHESIANS 2:8–9 NIV

✝ *Each of you should use whatever gift you have received to serve others, as faithful stewards of God's grace in its various forms.*

1 PETER 4:10 NIV

✝ *I long to see you so that I may impart to you some spiritual gift to make you strong—that is, that you and I may be mutually encouraged by each other's faith.*

ROMANS 1:11–12 NIV

October 8, 2019
1/3

Hey Pops —

You will not get this letter in the mail, but I am going to write it anyway. I got a call early this morning that I never saw coming. I woke at 2:00 AM CT to a call from Mom and she told me you had just passed away. I ran down the mosaic tile and hardwood floors of the house H and I just moved into, sobbing. I fell to the floor in a ball and cried out "this is not right", "I want to wake up," and "No... No... No." I bleated like a wounded animal as I hyperventilated and wept on the floor. I felt a level of grief I did not know was possible.

It has been just under 24 hours since that phone call. H and I flew to Atlanta with Mimi from San Antonio. We met Cory at the airport and rode to your and Mom's apartment together. We have cried, laughed, and loved today. We are doing everything we can to honor you and learn what happened. Tomorrow there will be an autopsy to confirm the cause of your death. At this point, we believe it was a thromboembolism (blood clot) or stress-induced heart attack. I am no medical doctor, but it seems your death was not cancer-related. If that is true, I am, in a way, thankful for your diagnosis of esophageal cancer. I hope this statement would not offend you; I will explain

I still feel the pain, heartbreak, and grief that crashed down on me this morning. But I am neither broken nor overwhelmed. I am so, incredibly thankful for the past months that we had to talk about faith and hope in the gospel. Had we not spent the last two months this way, I would not have witnessed your tremendous courage in facing your treatment and ~~would never have heard you~~ you never would have told me you were praying "Thy will be done" during your radiation treatments.

It is not going to be easy to move forward in this life without you. I will miss you every time I want career advice, every time I watch a sport event and want to text you about the score, every time I want to celebrate a success, and every time I need to be encouraged. A boy could not ask for a better father, only for more time with him. For reasons I don't understand, more time with you was not God's will for me. Maybe God's will was for us to fight this curse of the enemy together, to win the war while the enemy was focused on the battle.

Everyone misses you terribly and is hurting. All of our family is relying on me right now and if it were up to

JUST ME, I WOULD BE A TOTAL FAILURE.
BUT IT IS NOT UP TO ME ALONE. GOD IS
WITH ME AND HAS BEEN BUILDING ME UP EVER
SINCE YOUR DIAGNOSIS IN JULY. WITH GOD'S
STRENGTH, I AM GOING TO DO MY DUTY IN
GOD'S WILL WITH THE SAME COURAGE YOU
SHOWED OVER THE PAST MONTHS. I LOVE YOU,
I MISS YOU, AND I THANK YOU FOR EVERYTHING
YOU DID FOR ME.

WE FOUGHT TOGETHER;
TOGETHER, WE WON.
WITH A SON'S LOVE FOR
HIS FATHER,

CHAPTER EIGHTEEN

Spread Seeds

I NEVER GOT TO hear my father ring the bell again. He died in the early hours of October 8, 2019, from a pulmonary thromboembolism. I have since learned cancer patients, especially those undergoing treatment, are at an increased risk of developing blood clots. My father was one of the patients who developed them.

I will never forget what I saw when I got to my parents' apartment in Atlanta the day my father died. There were statements of faith and hope written all over the bathroom mirrors and glass walls of the shower. My father had proclaimed his trust in Christ. He was resting. He was home.

The Bible talks a lot about faith being like seeds. It says faith as small as a mustard seed can move a mountain, but also says most seeds never become anything. It says you harvest what you sow, but also says what grows from a seed is different from the seed planted. I never really understood these seed metaphors until my father died and I thought back about my life with him.

May 2000 – Dallas, Texas

I WAS TEN years old. It was my birthday. My parents took several of my friends and me to a medieval-themed jousting tournament and dinner. We sat in the stands drinking broth from stone bowls and cheering for the Red Knight, the champion of our section of the arena. Make-believe and medieval history were not in my father's wheelhouse, but that did not matter. He bought wooden replica swords, axes, and other medieval weapons for every kid in our group. We waved them overhead as we watched the faux battle rage below us. I looked over at my father and noticed he was not watching the show; he was watching me, and he was smiling.

Fall 2003 – Denver, Colorado

I WAS THIRTEEN years old. It was a late summer night after football practice. My coach had assigned me a new position, and I had spent the entire two hours of the practice getting my butt kicked and being tossed into the ground as I fought back tears of frustration under my helmet. My father was at practice, like always. As we walked to the car, he put his arm around me.

"You are a champion, son. You belong," he said. I knew he meant it. I knew he would stand there, on the edge of the field, and encourage me for as long as I wanted to keep going. He would never stop.

June 2008 – League City, Texas

I WAS EIGHTEEN years old. It was the summer after my high school graduation, just weeks before I moved out of the house. I was in the passenger seat of my father's pickup. We both knew it would be one of the last rides we would take together before I left for college. He pulled over next to the long stretch of white signs lining the road next to my high school.

"There it is," he said as he pointed to the sign with my name printed above the university I would be attending that fall.

"It's not a big deal, Dad. Most of the kids have a sign," I said.

"But no one else is going where you are," he said. That was true, as far as I knew, but I did not see the point. I was going to a regional liberal arts school. It was a good school, but most people had never heard of it. There were dozens of signs for Ivy League schools and prestigious universities with other kids' names on them. My father did not care. No sign was so impressive to him as the one with my name on it.

September 27, 2019 – Atlanta, Georgia

I WAS TWENTY-NINE years old. It was the day my father rang the bell, the last time I saw him. I was about to leave for my flight home to San Antonio. My mother was going to drive me to the airport while he rested. I was talking to my father as he sat on the couch when I saw it—the look he gave when he was about to assume control over the room and give a lecture. I stopped talking; I had learned better a long time ago.

"You and Hannah are about to be really successful," he said. He paused, looked away from me, and then looked back into my eyes. It was his trademark move, his way to show he had authority to control the room even with silence.

He continued, "I don't think you understand. Y'all are going to have options and opportunities to choose what kind of life y'all want." It was another of his trademark moves: telling people they were not paying enough attention to the wisdom he was delivering. I nodded to acknowledge him. He stared me in the eyes. "I am so proud of you, son. You have earned it. Don't be afraid when your opportunity comes."

The last thing my father told me was not to be afraid to be great.

MY FATHER SPENT twenty-nine years sowing seeds of love and encouragement into me; never once in my life did he tell me there was anything I could not do. A lot of the seed died because I was too ungrateful, headstrong, and arrogant for it to grow. But some of it took hold. And when the seed finally blossomed, it was different from what had been planted.

The seed was a father's love for his son, but the harvest was a son's love for his father. During my struggles as a child, my father gave me the encouragement and security only a father can give a son; during his battle with cancer, I told him he had the same encouragement and security from his Heavenly Father.

How terribly frustrating it must be for the enemy to witness this. How unfairly he must think the odds are stacked against him. To win the war, he must win every single battle. When we are like plants attached to God's roots, throwing seeds of faith, hope, and love out into the wind, the enemy must stop them all, for each individual seed that slips through and takes hold has the potential to release thousands of seeds itself. Each seed has even the ability to provide life back to the plant from which it came. The enemy wants a barren wasteland, but when we are rooted in God—when we are living on faith, hope, and love—we are an overgrown and fecund forest.

This book does not have a sad ending; it has a hopeful beginning. I have received a lot of seed in my life, more than my fair share of love and encouragement. For twenty-nine years, my father gave me the best of himself. Now, I carry the powerful potential of his love inside me. I am ready to spread it.

GOD'S WORD ABOUT THE FRUITS OF FAITH

✝ *He told them another parable: "The kingdom of heaven is like a mustard seed, which a man took and planted in his field. Though it is the smallest of all seeds, yet when it grows, it is the largest of garden plants and becomes a tree, so that the birds come and perch in its branches."*

MATTHEW 13:31–32 NIV

✝ *"But blessed is the one who trusts in the Lord,*
  whose confidence is in him.
They will be like a tree planted by the water
  that sends out its roots by the stream.
It does not fear when heat comes;
  its leaves are always green.
It has no worries in a year of drought
  and never fails to bear fruit."

JEREMIAH 17:7–8 NIV

✝ *And I heard a loud voice from the throne saying, "Look! God's dwelling place is now among the people, and he will dwell with them. They will be his people, and God himself will be with them and be their God. 'He will wipe every tear from their eyes. There will be no more death' or mourning or crying or pain, for the old order of things has passed away."*

REVELATION 21:3–4 NIV

My Eulogy for Pops

Delivered on October 19, 2019

MY DAD HAD several names. To family, he was John David. To my mom, he was just John or sometimes Babe. To friends, he was Zunk, JZ, or even —he claimed—"Zunk the Junk Yard Dog," although that was a little before my time, and I never actually heard anyone call him that.

To me, he was Dad until after I moved out of the house and started calling him Pops. You see, my dad and I butted heads when I was in high school. He wanted me to be a lawyer; I wanted to play lead guitar in a heavy metal band. It wasn't until after I left the house that I started to realize and say to myself, "Wow. My dad was right." My dad seemed wiser each year that I grew older. And "Pops" sounded like a wise name, so I started calling him that as a way to honor him. Mom never got a new name; she had always seemed wise to me.

I want to honor Pops today by sharing with everyone the greatest lesson he ever taught me. From July 29, the day of Pops' cancer diagnosis, through October 8, I wrote Pops seventeen letters to encourage him with the Good News and hope of the Gospel. In return, he taught me his greatest lesson, not by his words, but by his actions.

In Luke 9:23, Jesus instructs us to take up our cross daily and follow Him. But here's an important point: We don't get to pick *out* our cross; we just have to pick *up* our cross. We don't get to choose what challenges we face in life; we just get to choose whether we are going to overcome them in faith.

Pops' cross was a diagnosis of esophageal cancer at age fifty-four. That's not a pretty cross. But he chose to carry that cross with tremendous courage as he fought through his chemo and radiation treatments. I am not saying Pops was not scared; I know he was. But he chose courage over fear, hope over despair, and love over hate as he faithfully carried his cross through the end of his race. Many years ago, Pops told me the one thing no one could take from me was how I chose to respond to my situation. Following his cancer diagnosis, I reminded him of those words. I hope we choose to respond in our darkest hour as Pops did in his.

I want us to think about two crosses Pops did not have to bear. First, Pops' cross was not to waste away in bed, unable to move or work to provide for his family. Pops worked until 7:00 p.m. the night before he died. This may not sound to you like a great way to spend your last day. But to Pops, who placed the utmost value on providing for his family, it was extremely important.

Second, Pops' cross was not to grieve the deaths of his wife, sons, brother, or even parents. That is our cross. It's not pretty, but we don't get to choose what it looks like. All we get to choose is whether we are going to pick it up. And if you think you don't have the strength to pick that cross up today, I am here to tell you that you do. God will give you the strength. I have witnessed it firsthand, and let me tell you, a hideous cross faithfully carried becomes a beautiful thing. *That* is the greatest lesson Pops taught me.

I would like to close by praying for my mom, brother, uncle, grandparents, wife, and everyone else in this room.

God, we pray for the strength to tell the enemy, "Not today. Today is not the day we give in to despair. Today is not the day we curse God for our misfortune. Today is not the day we harden our hearts in hate. Today is not the day we lose hope. Not today."

God, lift us up. Help us see that John David's courageous fight against cancer was a beautiful example of how to faithfully carry our cross. Help us see that our cross to carry is this grief we feel, right here, right now. Help us see your outstretched hand is before us, offering all the assistance we need.

God, we proclaim your truth and goodness as a family of believers here today. When others say the world is bad because good things can be taken away, we say it is good because the best cannot. When others say John David is dead forever, we say he is at perfect rest in Your peace, waiting for the day he will be reborn in a glorious, cancer-free body.

Above all else, Heavenly Father, we pray that Thy will be done, today, tomorrow, and forever and ever, until the end of time and the beginning of an eternal, glorious present.

Amen.

Afterword

I FIRST MET KYLE in Houston, Texas on a long, June day in 1994. He was one of the first to join Mom and Pops in the delivery room. He beamed with joy as he looked over Mom's shoulder and saw me, his little brother, for the first time.

I have watched this scene unfold over and over when my family breaks out the old home movies from time to time as most families do. Nowadays, anytime I talk about my brother, I look a lot like that four-year-old version of Kyle from the home movies, beaming with pride and joy.

Kyle and I are very different people. It seems we inherited different parts of Mom and Pops, not divided along the line of good or bad, just different. I rather enjoy that aspect of our sibling relationship, and I deeply admire his approach to life.

The one thing Kyle and I have in common without a doubt is our amazing parents. We have both experienced the nurturing love of our sweet Mom and the stern but always affirming love of Pops.

When our Pops passed away, we lost a great man. I am lucky to have an older brother like Kyle, and while Pops might not be here, I can always look to Kyle as the role model in my life.

Pops' illness was fast and took him from us in a matter of months. In those months, we witnessed a man walk the walk of every lesson he ever taught us about being mentally tough and never feeling sorry for yourself. What we saw in those months was nothing short of heroic.

During this time, Kyle wrote to Pops about faith in seventeen letters. Those seventeen letters made a profound impact on Pops. There is no doubt in my mind, when Pops left the earthly world behind on October 8, 2019, those letters helped his spirit go in peace.

I will always be grateful for my brother and the letters he wrote that inspired this book.

CORY ZUNKER
June 16, 2021

In honor of Pops, my first hero, biggest fan,
and forever favorite partner in cards.

John David Zunker

September 8, 1964 – October 8, 2019

Acknowledgments

GETTING THIS BOOK out of my head, off of my desk, and into the world taught me a lot about humility. I needed the help of countless people. Fortunately, the world is full of passionate people who want to do good work and help each other. I owe gratitude to innumerable kind souls, including those who follow.

My beautiful bride, H—*Thank you for lighting up my life like fireworks on the beach. You shine golden rays of joy, and the world is a brighter place because of you.*

My sons, Finley and Ladd—*Thank you for teaching me about God's love and helping me become a little less selfish. I hope this book will help you know the grandfather you never met. Please always remember, you belong.*

Mom—*Thank you for always making me feel heard. I have never lived a day unsure of whether you love me.*

Cory—*Thank you for giving me the special bond of brotherhood. I see Pops in you more and more each day.*

Grandpa Tony, Granny and Papaw, Mimi and Jim, Papa John and Lydia—*Thank you for spoiling me with love. Being the first grandchild to seven grandparents was a rare privilege for which I am grateful.*

Davey J—*Thank you for always helping me get across the finish line, including with this book.*

Dr. J—*Thank you for helping me sift through the broken pieces to find this book. Without you, there would be no Amazing Courage.*

Jen, Bill, Akemi, and the team at StoryBuilders—*Thank you for making me feel like more than a client. You are elite at your craft but even better people.*

Elizabeth, Jeremy, and the team at Brand Builders Group—*Thank you for teaching me a lot where I knew very little.*

Karla and Julie —*Thank you for believing in my book when the metrics of the industry labeled me a nobody.*

PB, Heather, and the team at Pearl Street Church—*Thank you for saving my life. I can never repay the debt I owe to your ministry.*

Pastor Josh, Amber, and the team at One Hope Church—*Thank you for giving my family a home away from home in New Orleans.*

Finally, I would like to thank my aunts, uncles, and cousins for helping to shape me; my good friends for celebrating the best in me and putting up with the worst; my family-by-marriage for welcoming me with genuine love and open arms; my teachers, professors, and coaches for helping me grow; and my law firm, Cokinos | Young, for giving me a chance to be great.

About the Author

KYLE ZUNKER IS a leading construction attorney, former atheist, and the author of *Amazing Courage*, a book about the power to choose faith over fear.

As a principal of one of Texas' largest construction-focused law firms, Kyle has represented national and international construction companies in numerous multi-million-dollar disputes. His work on these high-stakes legal cases has resulted in seven- and eight-figure damage awards and his recognition in Best Lawyers: Ones to Watch® in America in the field of Construction Law. His expertise is backed by his Doctor of Jurisprudence, *magna cum laude*, from Southern Methodist University's Dedman School of Law and his triple-major Bachelor of Arts in philosophy, English, and Spanish, also *magna cum laude*, from Texas Lutheran University. As a leader in his industry, he serves as the Young Lawyer's Representative for the Construction Section of the State Bar of Texas and hosts the Basic Course in Texas Construction Law.

Kyle finds meaning in conquering ultra-distance endurance athletics events. In 2021, he completed the Leadville 100 Trail Run—a 100-mile footrace across the

Rocky Mountains—and raised more than $12,500 for charity in the process. He followed that up in 2023 by running the Habanero Hundred—a 100-mile footrace in the dog days of Texas's legendary summer heat, with temperatures reaching 107 degrees Fahrenheit. Kyle passionately supports his local churches in New Orleans and San Antonio through financial giving and by serving on the advisory board, where his legal training and goal-oriented practical experience provide valuable insight.

As a former atheist, Kyle struggled with fear, anxiety, and panic attacks. His life changed when he chose faith and learned to fight fear's lies with God's truth. When his father was diagnosed with esophageal cancer a few years later, Kyle put the lessons he learned into practice by writing letters of encouragement to his father throughout his treatment. He now seeks to help others overcome their fears through faith in action.